UNQUENCHABLE LOVE

David & Heather
Kopp

Cover by Koechel-Peterson & Associates, Minneapolis, Minnesota

UNQUENCHABLE LOVE

Copyright © 1999 by David and Heather Kopp
Published by Harvest House Publishers
Eugene, Oregon 97402

Library of Congress Cataloging-in-Publication Data

Kopp, David, 1949-
    Unquenchable love / David and Heather Kopp.
       p. cm.
    ISBN 1-56507-821-7
    1. Spouses—Prayer-books and devotions—English. 2. Marriage—Religious aspects—Christianity. 3. Love—Religious aspects—Christianity. 4. Marriage—Biblical teaching. 5. Love—Biblical teaching.
    I. Kopp, Heather Harpham, 1964- . II. Title.
    BV4596.M3K66 1999
    242'.644—dc21
                                       98-47207
                                            CIP

Printed in the United States of America.

99   00   01   02   03   04   /   DH   /   10   9   8   7   6   5   4   3   2   1

Special thanks to
Kristen Ingram Johnson and Nancy Kennedy

CONTENTS

Couples You Want to Know

"Many waters cannot quench love;
 rivers cannot wash it away.
If one were to give all the wealth
 of his house for love, it would
 be utterly scorned."

—SONG OF SONGS 8:7

Couples
You Want to Know

If you could ask your favorite married couples in the Bible—beginning with Adam and Eve and ending with Joseph and Mary—to stop by your kitchen for a visit, would you? What if, one by one, you could ask them your deepest questions or share your disappointments and fondest dreams about married love?

If you're like us, you probably grew up hearing about these husbands and wives—only to leave them stuck on the flannel graph of your childhood or tripping around a church stage in borrowed bathrobes.

But if we go back and look carefully at God's love stories, we discover real women and men experiencing marriage in ways we all recognize—and in ways we can all learn from. Who better to teach us about wielding power in a relationship than Esther and Xerxes? Who better to give us lessons on romance than the Lover and the Beloved of the Song of Songs? And what might Jacob—that dreamer and schemer—have to say to us about the cost of love?

After two years of research on these couples, we wrote a book called *Love Stories God Told*. Our mission was to retell biblical love stories in a way that answered the question, "Does God care really about romantic love?"

For this book, we wanted to revisit these couples in order to look more deeply into the marriage principles that God wants to teach us through their stories. Over the course of 12 weeks of personal or group study, you'll meet some inspiring (and surprising) marriage mentors from God's Word. A study guide at the back is designed for use in a group or just between you and your spouse—over dinner or across the pillow—to promote the kind of heart-to-heart conversations that make any love relationship blossom.

We believe God included each love and marriage story in the Bible for important reasons. He cares about your heart and your marriage commitments. We pray that each story will bring you timeless truths and practical encouragement for a new love story God wants to tell—yours.

—David and Heather Kopp
SISTERS, OREGON

Unquenchable Love

CHAPTER ONE

Adam & Eve

About Adam

Name: Means "of the ground"

Age at Marriage: Probably corresponded physically to an 18-25-year-old

Appearance: The ultimate man, reflecting the beautiful possibilities of all the races to come

Personality: Unknown, but he was the prototype for all humans

Family Background: No father or mother besides God, his Maker

Place in History: First man; famous for causing sin to enter the world by eating the forbidden fruit offered to Eve

About Eve

Name: Means "the life-giving one"

Age at Marriage: Probably corresponded physically to a 16-22-year-old

Appearance: Traditionally considered the most beautiful woman who ever lived

Personality: Like Adam, unknown

Family Background: No parents, made from Adam's rib; "born" into a marriage

Place in History: Last being God personally created; famous for succumbing to the serpent and eating the forbidden fruit of Eden

Discovering the Meaning of Marriage

Genesis 2-3

"In the beginning . . ." God made a lot of stuff out of nothing, and kept a checklist as he went along:

> Day and night—*"good"* (especially during June).
>
> Plants—*"good"* (consider strawberries, say, or a redwood tree . . .)
>
> Birds and fish—*"good"* (colors, sounds, and shapes like you've never imagined)
>
> Animals, both wild and tame—*"good"* (yes, but did He notice the gnu?)
>
> Man—*"good"* (after morning coffee and a shave anyway)

Everything looks good in Eden until halfway through chapter two of Genesis. There, God starts handing out the assignments. He gives Adam a job to do (take care of the garden), lots of freedom (to eat anything he wants), and one restriction (*don't* eat from the tree of the knowledge of good and evil).

And then for the first time, God hesitates. "It is *not good* for the man to be alone," He says. "I will make a helper suitable for him" (verse 18).

Preachers have a lot of fun with this sequence. When God needed a man to get something done right, they say, He went looking for a woman.

God may have gone looking for a "suitable helper," but what He came away with was more than another good creation to add to the list. God put Adam into a deep sleep and made a woman from one of his ribs. When He finished, He brought her to Adam.

What did Adam see when he opened his eyes? He saw himself—and more, much more—looking back at him. It was the moment of the first heart thump, the first crush, the first human longing . . .

In this amazing passage (Genesis 2:18-24) God went beyond the physical universe on which most creation stories focus. Here, he imagined and then made the human universe that matters so much to us every day. In one sweep, God:

- Created a woman to complete the man (friendship).
- Completed the creation of humans—together, male and female reflect "his own image" (wholeness).
- Brought man and woman together (sexual and spiritual union).
- Gave the man and woman an immediate task (homemaking and family).
- Created a future for the human race (procreation).

What does this spectacular sweep add up to? Marriage—the only human institution created by God before the fall.

No one knows if there was a wedding ceremony in the Garden that day (we do know there was no wedding dress). But Adam and Eve became the world's first married couple. In fact, Eve never knew what it meant to be single; she was essentially created married.

For couples trying to understand the promise and possibilities of God's plan for marriage, the story of Adam and Eve makes a great beginning. Here, you'll find answers to basic questions about marriage: Where did it come from? What is it for? Why do people want it, anyway? Is it good?

Key phrases pop up in the poetry of Genesis, phrases that have become part of Christian wedding vows: "be fruitful" (1:28), "not good for a man to be alone" (2:18), "a helper" (2:18), "bone of my bone and flesh of my flesh" (2:23), "leave . . . father and mother" (2:24), "become one flesh" (2:24). Each phrase is a window into God's intentions for a man and a woman in love.

But it's hard to talk about the wonders of love in Eden without also facing the tragedies of sin that followed. And you thought *The Lucille Ball Show* or *Mad About You* made history with one marital mix-up after another? Read Genesis 3. It took a husband and a wife just one afternoon to sink God's entire plan.

Happily, the story doesn't stop there. In the new, thorn-choked world, marriage bonds became even more important. In fact, maybe God was thinking ahead when he put so much emphasis on the marriage partnership. Antoine de Saint-Exupéry wrote, "To love does not mean simply to look at one another but to look together in the same direction." We were made for each other, and love makes us one and it makes us strong.

These days when the idea of marriage gets so complicated— even meaningless to some—it's good to rediscover the miracle that survived the closing of Eden's gates. In the arms of each other, in the children we bear, in our home and family, and in the long, intimate friendship of man and wife, we can reexperience some of the wholeness of Eden.

God's name for that miracle is married love. And it is very good.

Then the Lord God made a woman from the rib he had taken out of the man, and he brought her to the man. The man said, "This is now bone of my bones and flesh of my flesh; she shall be called 'woman,' for she was taken out of man." For this reason a man will leave his father and mother and be united to his wife, and they will become one flesh.

—GENESIS 2:22-24

1 *Blind Love*

As Adam gazed at the woman God had made for him, he uttered the first human words ever recorded—"Bones of my bone and flesh of my flesh . . ."

What do you hear in those words? Wonder? Recognition? Delight? Commitment? Maybe all these and more—which is probably what God had in mind. Because immediately after the couple were formally introduced, God revealed what he was really up to on that most amazing day in Eden. In the next sentence, God created the institution of marriage:

"For this reason, a man shall leave his father and his mother and be united to his wife . . ."

God had already created two of each of all the animals, female and male. Interestingly, there's no hint that these female animals were made *from* the males. And only in the case of humans did God institute the relationship of marriage. Why?

God intended that this union of male and female would involve more than companionship (cows do that), mating pleasure (butterflies have that), or lifetime cohabiting (geese hold the record there). As husband and wife, we express a mysterious and spiritual union—one flesh. It's the arithmetic of heaven: one plus one equals one!

16

With this amazing proclamation of oneness (Genesis 2:24), God performs the "wedding" of Adam and Eve. In the next sentence, Eve is called Adam's wife.

Throughout history people have tried to explain marriage—why man and woman experience the "urge to merge." They've analyzed marriage in terms of culture, biology, security, child-rearing, and economics. They've gone to the polls and to the courts to decide which of us (and in what gender combinations) get to call ourselves "married."

But the wonderful truth is that marriage was God's idea from the start. He never asked for anyone else's opinion on the matter. *Be completed,* He said on that wedding day in the Garden. *Be united. Be delighted!*

God didn't just create marriage and walk away, either. Genesis tells us that God provided for the new couple's needs (2:7-9), gave them purpose and guidance (2:15-18), and provided His own presence for companionship (3:8). Even when they failed terribly, He kept showing them His tender love (3:21; 4:1).

When we enter into marriage, we recapture a glimpse of Eden. *God continues to be the Creator of every marriage where He is the honored guest—not just at the ceremony, but through every day of our lives.* (Who is more aware than God that, without Him, we're spouting impossible vows when we kneel at the altar?)

The God of Eden is the Lord of husbands and wives today. He alone knows the mysterious and incredible possibilities of a married man and woman. He alone knows how to make two hearts add up to the miracle number: *one.*

> *Creator Lord,*
> *Thank You for the marriage miracle. Thank You that marriage isn't a fad or a cultural preference but a lasting, divine, and holy covenant that You created for our good. Thank You for creating my other half to*

lovingly complete me. Remind me all day that my marriage is a gift from You and is part of Your highest purpose for my life. Amen.

 How could understanding that marriage was God's idea—that He created *your* marriage—help you deal with difficulties today?

When God created man, he created him in
the likeness of God. He created them male and
female and blessed them. And when they were
created, he called them "man."
—GENESIS 5:1-2

2 *Male & Female*

If it took both male and female to encompass the "likeness of God," why did God make Adam first, and *then* Eve?

Rabbis of old taught that God created Eve so that Adam would understand that he was not God's equal. Some scholars propose that Eve was actually the pinnacle of God's creative genius. All that hoopla about the naming of the animals, they say, was like one long drum roll leading up to God's crowning achievement.

One thing Scripture makes clear is that in a world untouched by sin, where Adam literally "had it all," he still needed a woman. By taking a rib from Adam's body, God showed His intention of making woman from the place closest to man's heart. The man recognized that woman had come from him, and for a time the two had perfect harmony.

Then sin introduced conflict between Adam and Eve. Maybe this was part of the serpent's plan all along—to set God's beloved children at odds with each other. And it worked. When God asked Adam what had gone wrong, he blamed Eve: "The woman you put here with me—she gave me some fruit from the tree, and I ate it" (Genesis 3:12).

Moments later, God told Eve that because of her disobedience she would be "ruled" by her husband. "Your desire will be for your husband, and he will rule over you" (Genesis 3:16).

The first couple's first conflict set the war of the sexes in motion. As man and wife, we experience something of it every day, no matter how in love we are. Why? First, because we're influenced by self and by sin. And second because we're different. Not better or worse, not more or less valuable, just different—physically and emotionally.

It's a set up for conflict, and for one-liners like: "Behind every successful man in the world is a woman who couldn't be more surprised," and "Men say women can't be trusted too far; women say men can't be trusted too near."

The genders God made *do* seem uniquely gifted: He competes; she comforts. He strives for individual accomplishment; she strives for mutual understanding. He protects; she nurtures. He builds; she furnishes.

Generalizations like these are always limited (and invitations for more warfare). But the good news is that the differences between men and women are both a blessing and an opportunity. As Antonio Machado advises, "Look for your other half who walks always next to you and tends to be who you aren't."

Through working together—especially in marriage—we can become *more* than just male and female. As we are tender with each other's weaknesses, as we delight in each other's strengths, as we learn to admire each other's uniquenesses (seeing God's lavish creativity in the other person)—we can become the beautiful sum of our differences.

And more like the beautiful image of God.

Lord and Maker,

Thank You for making us male and female. Today I pray that You would help us both to make the most of Your plan. Show us each how to understand what it's like to be a man or a woman. Help us to teach each other gently, and to work at compensating and complementing instead of competing. In Your name we pray, Amen.

Tell each other what is the best and the worst thing about being male or female. Identify one way that you might be able to turn a gender difference into an opportunity today.

To the woman he said, "I will greatly increase your pains in childbearing; with pain you will give birth to children. Your desire will be for your husband, and he will rule over you." To Adam he said, ". . . Cursed is the ground because of you; through painful toil you will eat of it all the days of your life. It will produce thorns and thistles for you . . ."

—GENESIS 3:16-18

3 Fallout from the Fall

At first glance, it appears that the consequences of the Fall were intended by God to further separate the genders and their roles. But in reality, God was setting up a means for survival in a harsh new world where Adam and Eve would need each other more than ever. Whereas once life in Eden had been easy, and romance came as naturally as laughter, now the two had to work at everything, including love.

Sound familiar? To this day, when we discover ourselves tumbling happily into love, we experience a slice of Eden. Everything seems perfect. Our beloved miraculously completes us. But as time passes, we seem to eat from the tree of knowledge. Our eyes are opened to our lover's quirks and shortcomings.

Even in an instant world of internet access and drive-up lattes, we recognize the fallout from the Fall: Making a living is hard work. Bearing children is painful and exhausting. Everything that really matters seems to be surrounded by thorns. And then we return to the dust. . . .

How much we need our beloved "other half" just to make it! And this is what God had in mind. In fact, Adam and Eve's best hope for survival—and for the survival of the human race—was to stick together and share the load. Imagine if Adam had been so disappointed in Eve's foolishness that he'd stomped off into the woods. Or if Eve had refused to ever make love again with such an arrogant, blameshifting creature as Adam.

After the Fall, love wasn't just a nice option; it was essential. In this sometimes hostile environment, it is clear that God had even larger plans for marriage. He wanted the marital bond to provide the passion, safety, and mutual commitment necessary for bearing and raising children. "Be fruitful and increase in number," God told His new world (Genesis 1:28).

Marriage is not so much about learning to embrace the hard work of life as it is about embracing each other—and watching the work get a little easier. That is why God made marriage to be practical.

When Solomon contemplated the vanities of the fallen world, he saw hope in committed relationships: "Two are better than one, because they have a good return for their work: If one falls down, his friend can help him up . . . If two lie down together, they will keep warm. But how can one keep warm alone? Though one may be overpowered, two can defend themselves" (Ecclesiastes 4:9-12).

What are some practical ways we can try to compensate for the fallout from the Fall in our marriage today? Let's look at Solomon's insights:

- A good return (verse 9)—What kind of efficiencies could we realize through clearly drawn expectations and separation of duties? How can we take advantage of "two"?

- Help (verse 10)—Has one of us needed help lately? Is there a "ditch" one or both of us keep falling into? How can we prepare in advance for these times of need?

- Warmth (verse 11)—Do I understand what comfort feels like to my spouse? Is it something I do, say, or provide? Where could emotional warmth make a big difference right now?

- Defense (verse 12)—What enemy (or enemies) are we facing right now? Have we been honest with our spouse about what we really fear? How could we go on the defensive for each other and our marriage today?

Anyone can have a heyday with marriage problems (just listen in on the conversation in any coffee shop or turn on any TV talk show). But today we can celebrate the wisdom of God's plan for marriage. *"Two are better than one . . ."*

Standing side by side, we can enjoy love's blessings and find new strength to face our world together. And we can hear God exclaim again, "It is good!"

> *Creator Lord,*
>   *Today I am reminded just how much I need my mate. Thank You that the first love story You told didn't end when sin entered. Thank You that You did not abandon Adam and Eve, nor they each other. Teach me how to work together with my mate so that we can overcome the challenges of life by Your strength and our love. Amen.*

Love Talk

A surprising number of the minuses of marriage fade away if we focus on making the most of the pluses. Spend time with Solomon's advice today. Do you have a "marriage plus" you're both overlooking?

*Then the eyes of both of them were opened, and
they realized they were naked; so they sewed fig
leaves together and made coverings for themselves.*
—GENESIS 3:7

*He answered, "I heard you in the garden, and I
was afraid because I was naked; so I hid."*
—GENESIS 3:10

*And the LORD God made garments of skin for
Adam and his wife and clothed them.*
—GENESIS 3:21

4 "Naked but Found"

One of the saddest consequences of the Fall in Eden was Adam and Eve's realization that they were naked. They both felt shame for the first time. Shame is a deep sense of not being accepted—"As a person, I'm not OK."

Their first impulse was to hide—and not just their bodies, but themselves—from God. But of course God found them. And His response reveals that his love for Adam and Eve was stronger than their disobedience. He didn't rip away their silly leaves in a fit of anger, but made garments Himself for them to wear.

One of the sacred privileges of marriage is that we allow only our mate to see, and hopefully embrace, our nakedness. It's not just physical intimacy that we long for, but a spiritual and relational one. Often, it's even harder to be "naked" in front of our spouses with our souls, than with our bodies ("Admit to him my deepest, least attractive fears?" "Pray in front of my wife?")

We're invited to exercise a kind of priestly role with each other:

- We witness numerous and repeated blunders.

- We understand each other's intentions and regrets.

- We cover one another's sin by expressing our forgiveness.

- We remind each other of God's enduring affection,
  above and beyond anything we could do or say.

Sometimes in marriage, we discover that our spouse is still using fig leaves to hide behind. Fear, shame, or a sense of failure has taken over. That's when we get to say with God, "You may be naked, but you are not alone. I have found you out and I still want you. I will give you the covering of my love."

In a Christian marriage, we can experience openness and vulnerability, but we don't have to feel the fear of nakedness. We can be who we are—who Christ is in the process of making us every day—but we never have to feel shame. Not in front of our Maker. Not in front of our lover.

Because love knows us—and covers us completely.

Every day since Eden, wives and husbands have sinned in big and small ways. In your marriage today, when you have every right to judge or erupt in anger or bring shame, what covering of grace could you bring instead?

> *Lord and Maker,*
> *Thank You that You know everything about us and yet love us even more than we love one another. We praise You that You made marriage to be a sacred place where we could be more fully known, and where we could find reprieve from shame. Today, help us to learn to embrace each other when we feel exposed, ashamed, or foolish. Help us be willing to be open with one another in both body and soul. May we risk, and generously reward the risks, that intimacy requires. In Jesus name we humbly pray. Amen.*

 Love Talk | Recall a time when you felt especially exposed to your mate, and he or she accepted you as you were. Share these memories with one another before you go to sleep tonight.

*So they are no longer two, but one. There-
fore what God has joined together, let man not
separate.*

—Jesus (MATTHEW 19:6)

5 What God Has Joined

It's easy to miss the real lover in Genesis. In many ways the story of Adam and Eve is the love story of the Creator with His creation. God walks with Adam and Eve in the cool of the day, delighting in their company.

And after they have eaten the forbidden fruit, He calls out, "Where are you?" In His anguished question, we hear echoes of "Why aren't you here to share our time together? Something terrible is keeping us apart."

God has been betrayed. Stood up. The prophet Hosea described God's feelings as a jilted lover: "What can I do with you, Judah? Your love is like the morning mist, like the early dew that disappears. Like Adam, (you) have broken the covenant—(you) were unfaithful to me . . ." (Hosea 6:4,7).

God decided to take the risk of offering His children a choice, the risk that the beings He created in His image might choose disobedience instead of love. The consequences of their choice would rock all God's creation.

Yet when Adam and Eve failed, God had mercy on them. His words to them were more a sad and bleak report than an angry reaction. Instead of shaming Adam and Eve, He clothes them.

And when He banishes them from Eden, His purpose is to keep them from living on forever in their ruined state.

Down through time, the Lover of Eden has continued to pursue the human race. Just read the Bible and you'll see the record of His passion and persistence. In the New Testament, we discover the culmination of God's pursuit. Paul described it this way, "God demonstrates his own love for us in this: While we were still sinners, Christ died for us" (Romans 5:8).

Every day, God is still in full pursuit of each one of us—His special creations. The first business of every husband and wife is to receive God's love personally. His love is the real thing. He can rescue us from our sinful natures and foolish pasts, and give us new life eternally.

Then, as Christian husbands and wives, we can receive and respond to God's active presence in our marriages. "A cord of three strands is not quickly broken," wrote Solomon (Ecclesiastes 4:12). The promise of God's unfailing presence is the secret to a successful Christian marriage and the best wedding gift we'll ever receive.

The prophet Malachi described God's tenacious attitude toward marriage this way: ". . . the LORD is acting as the witness between you and the wife of your youth. . . . Has not the LORD made [you] one? In flesh and spirit [you] are his" (Malachi 2:14-15).

We must decide what to do with this "third party" in our love affair. We could hide. Or run. Or even disobey. But then we'd miss out on the fulfillment and peace of simply seeking the Lord together every day.

Through prayer, through listening for His voice in the Word, through spending time together in His presence and trying our best to obey Him, we can experience the marriage God has in mind for us.

Lord of Married Lovers,

Be here in our marriage today. Walk with us (help us to walk with You). Cover us with Your saving grace. Thank You for joining us together, and joining with us in this marriage journey. May nothing separate us, Lord. With praise and thanks we pray. Amen.

 The poet Robert Greene called love "the power divine that reigns in us." Is there something visible you could do today to tell the Lord, "You are present here, and You reign as King!" (Ideas—a written verse or prayer on the bathroom mirror, a candle buning during dinner; placing your wedding picture on top of a Bible in the kitchen just for the day.)

CHAPTER TWO

The Patriarchs

About Noah

Name: Means "rest"

Appearance: Unknown

Personality: Gifted with incredible perseverance;
willing to stand alone; a righteous man,
blameless . . . , he walked with God" (Genesis 6:9)

Age at Marriage: Unknown; according to Genesis
he was 600 years old at the time of the flood,
and lived to be 950

Family Background: Grandson of Methuselah,
who lived to be 969

Place in History: The man who built the ark and,
with his wife and family, survived the flood

About Noah's Wife

Name: Almost nothing is known about her, not even
her name

Place in History: The woman who stood by her husband
during the greatest cataclysm in history

Their Wives

About Abraham

Name: Means "father of a multitude"

Age at Marriage: Probably about 20; became a father at 100

Appearance: Unknown

Personality: Distinguished by his radical trust in God

Family Background: Grew up in Babylonia about 2000 B.C.; his father was Terah

Place in History: The first patriarch of the Jewish nation; father of Isaac; the pilgrim and man of faith whom God called "friend" (Isaiah 41:8); Paul called him "the father of all who believe" (Romans 4:11)

About Sarah

Name: Means "a princess"

Age at Marriage: Probably in her teens

Appearance: One of the Bible's great beauties

Personality: Pragmatic, enduring

Family Background: Like Abraham, originally from Ur in Babylonia

Place in History: The elderly wife who laughed when God said she would get pregnant—at 90, she gave birth to Isaac

Noah, Abraham, & Moses

About Moses

Name: Means "drawn out of"; given to him by Pharoah's daughter who said, "I drew him out of the water" (Exodus 2:10)

Age at Marriage: 40

Appearance: Unknown; traditionally presented as very commanding, with an intense gaze

Personality: Brooding, highly intelligent, humble, hot-tempered

Family Background: A Levite born into slavery in Egypt; grew up in Pharoah's court, but fled to deserts near Sinai after he murdered an Egyptian who was attacking a Jew (Exodus 2:11-15)

Place in History: The man who led the Jews out of Egyptian slavery and received the Law from God at Mt. Sinai; considered the founder of Judaism

About Zipporah

Name: Means "swallow"

Age at Marriage: Probably in her late teens

Appearance: Unknown

Personality: Scholar Merrill Unger writes, "seems to have been prejudiced and rebellious and of little help to her husband."

Family Background: A Midianite from the Mt. Sinai/Red Sea area; her father Jethro was an adviser to Moses

Place in History: The wife who performed an emergency circumcision on their son to save Moses' life

Moving Forward in Faith

Noah: Genesis 6–9
Abraham: Genesis 11,12,17,18
Moses: Exodus 2–4

Maybe what God missed most about Eden were those walks in the evening. Remember? "The man and his wife heard the sound of the LORD God as he was walking in the garden in the cool of the day" (Genesis 3:8).

But one very bad day ruined all that.

One way to look at the Bible story after the Fall is that God is trying—through His divine dealings with us—to get back to those garden walks. Down through the ages, and right into our own lives, God keeps pursuing a relationship with us, His people. "God is always coming, and we, like Adam, hear His footsteps," writes Carlo Carretto. "God comes because God is love, and love needs to give of itself. God has always been coming; God is always coming."

But humans are nearly always running away. Through angry, sinful rebellion, they keep trying to make the distance between themselves and God as great as possible. In this chapter, we'll look at some who didn't—three husbands and wives who chose to walk with God, and whom God used in extraordinary times.

We'll also look at some of the most catastrophic events in earth's history. But in every roar of water or thunder of chariots, there's really only one sound to remember. It is the quiet footsteps of the Lord of love coming closer to His people.

What He brings with Him, in each of these stories from Genesis and Exodus, is a covenant. Like our own marriage covenant, these are vows of relationship. And like our promises to each other, God's promises of how He will deal with us are based on a personal guarantee, not on the other party's performance.

Each promise begins with a picture.

Rainbows. By the time of Noah, only a dozen generations after Adam, "every inclination of the thoughts of his [man's] heart was only evil all the time" (Genesis 6:5). So God decided to start over with one family—Mr. and Mrs. Noah, along with their three married sons.

Why them? The Bible says, "Noah was a righteous man, blameless among the people of his time, and he walked with God" (Genesis 6:9). Even so, surely every fiber of Mr. and Mrs. Noah's convictions were tested almost beyond endurance by the catastrophe they lived through.

The Great Flood loosed an apocalypse on the earth like none before or since. It is impossible to imagine the devastation. But Noah and his family were carried safely through it, along with enough wildlife to start over. When the waters receded, God said the rainbow would be a sign of His promise that He would never destroy the earth again with water.

To this day, the rainbow is a symbol of hope. In our marriages, God's covenant to Noah brings confidence that as we walk with Him, we will be assured of God's unfailing goodness.

Stars. Soon after the earth is repopulated, the human race again slides into rebellion and idolatry. This time, God focuses not just on one family, but on an entire lineage who will become His chosen nation.

God calls Abraham and his wife, Sarah, away from their home in Mesopotamia and leads them to Canaan, a land that He will give them. "I will make you into a great nation and I will bless you" (Genesis 12:2). Over the years, God reiterates His promises to Abraham again and again: The promised land will be given to him, and he will have many descendants.

God invites Abraham to gaze up into the night sky. "Look up at the heavens and count the stars—if indeed you can count them," He says. "So shall your offspring be" (Genesis 15:5). But is this an empty promise? Everyone wants a piece of Abraham's land, and his wife is 90 years old and childless. What gives?

When time has long run out, Isaac, the "child of promise," is born. Then Abraham lives to see Isaac and Rebekah bear twins, Jacob and Esau. One by one, the stars begin to come out, just as God had promised.

Milk and honey. Genesis closes with Abraham's descendants living in Egypt, where they have gone to escape famine. But gradually the Pharoahs turn them into a slave race. The Jews groan in their chains, dreaming of Canaan, the "land of milk and honey" God had promised Abraham. Then God brings Moses onto the scene (Exodus 1–4). It is time for God's people to go home.

Moses arrives on the scene with a spotty record. Yes, he had grown up in Pharoah's court (Exodus 2), but he had murdered an Egyptian and fled to the desert where he lived for 40 years. When he returns, it is with a Midianite wife named Zipporah.

But God tells Moses, "I am sending you. "Tell the Israelites, God says, 'I am the LORD, and I will bring you out from under the yoke of the Egyptians . . . I will take you as my own people, and I will be your God'" (from Exodus 6:6-7).

The deliverance under Moses' leadership is called the Exodus. In the desert, God reveals His next covenant with His people— the Ten Commandments and other laws. By the time they arrive at the borders of the Promised Land, Israel has a much clearer understanding of what it means to be God's own people and to walk closely with Him.

What did the men and women of this epic era have in common? Notice that they began their extraordinary callings in ordinary marriages. Noah's wife, Sarah, and Zipporah—all these women thought they'd married an average Joe (was God smiling?).

But we discover a quality these men shared. They walked with God and listened to His voice. (Keep in mind there was no Bible, no church, no Jewish "religion" at this time.) And they had the audacity to believe, and act on the belief, that the God of the universe could be trusted—period.

The Bible word for this world-shaking conviction is *faith*. It's like a narrow footbridge—suspended high, swaying, but firm—between ordinary men and women and God's extraordinary plans and promises.

In the psalms, David looks up at the stars and wonders, "What is man that you are mindful of him?" (Psalm 8:4). Abraham and Sarah would answer, "The stars remind us that He *does* think of us."

In this chapter we'll discover:

- How as we covenant together with God, He will disclose to us a greater destiny than either of us could have imagined.

- How both of us are necessary to God's big plan for each of us.

- How God wants to lead us away from all kinds of doubts and fears, and toward the fulfillment He promises every couple when we reach for it in faith.

- How we can have a marriage called out from the world and set apart by obedience. God's purpose is always the same: He wants us for His own.

The story of our own marriages most likely won't include the same kinds of catastrophes or crises as these three. Or end up as a movie starring Charles Heston. But the story of each of our marriages is an epic that God wants to tell in heaven. The happy ending is just across that footbridge of faith.

I am going to bring floodwaters on the earth
to destroy all life under the heavens, every crea-
ture that has the breath of life in it. . . . But I
will establish my covenant with you, and you
will enter the ark—you and your sons and your
wife and your sons' wives with you.
—God speaks to Noah (GENESIS 6:17-18)

1 Faith Floats

This one's for the kids in Sunday school, right?

A smiling man named Mr. Noah builds a great big boat. He and Mrs. Noah and the kids collect birds and animals of every description—*Johnny, can you make the sound of an elephant? Krissy, how about the sound of a duck?*

Noah lines up the zoo, two by two, and leads the animals into the ark. The rain starts, the water rises and rises, and the big boat floats. After a long, scary ride, a dove brings back a branch, a sign of dry times ahead. Soon Noah will be watching the animals walk away. *Billy, can you make the sound of an elephant walking through the mud?*

As Noah and his happy family tell God "thank You," a pretty rainbow appears in the sky. "It's my promise," says God, "that when I get upset again, I won't drown everybody." *OK, class, let's color rainbows. . . .*

The kids go home, happy to know the truth about rainbows. But what about you? Try reading Genesis 6–9:17 aloud together on a rainy night, not as a story of a menagerie but a marriage. You'll notice that the colors and the sound effects fade. And you'll run right into a storm:

- A husband who buries himself (and his family) for decades in an absurd and all-consuming task.

- A wife who must endure years of humiliation—*Your husband is building a what?*

- An apocalypse of terror, drownings, chaos, and mass destruction.

- A year cooped up in a stinking, mall-sized animal pen.

- A 300-year-long old age with no neighbors to visit and a case of bad nerves every time it starts to rain.

That's the grown-up story.

In the face of that, we have to wonder exactly *who* Mr. and Mrs. Noah are. Are they calm, confident, and smiling—like those colorful cartoons we saw in children's books? Or are they huddled in the drippy darkness, questioning, often in despair, sometimes screaming, holding on by their fingernails—like they would be if we were them?

The Bible doesn't give a clear portrait of this couple, but it continually reassures us about one thing: *God can and does use people whether they feel happy or not, fearful or not.* Moses was terrified of speaking publicly (Exodus 4:10-13). Paul often used phrases like "under great pressure," "despaired even of life," "perplexed," and "sorrowful" to describe his turbulent emotions (2 Corinthians 1:8; 4:8; 6:10).

In the book of Hebrews, we find a clue as to how God views faith and feelings: "And without faith it is impossible to please God, because anyone who comes to him must believe that he exists and that he rewards those who earnestly seek him. By faith

Noah, when warned about things not yet seen, in holy fear built an ark to save his family" (Hebrews 11:6-7).

What God requires isn't nice, happy feelings, but the choice to act on faith. If we answer God's call because we hold Him in awe ("holy fear"), He promises to keep us in His ark of safety when the floodwaters rise. We can be screamers or smilers. Either way, we're welcome on board.

> Lord,
>   Sometimes our marriage feels like a man and a woman in cramped and soggy quarters, waiting for blue skies. Let faith make us strong today, no matter what we're feeling. In Jesus' name we pray. Amen.

 Love Talk | Discuss "the weather" in your home of late. Is it sunny? Dark? Wet for weeks? How can you help each other as you wait for dry land?

[Abraham] said to his wife Sarai, "I know what a beautiful woman you are. When the Egyptians see you, they will say, 'This is his wife.' Then they will kill me but will let you live. Say you are my sister, so that I will be treated well for your sake and my life will be spared because of you."

—GENESIS 12:11-13

2 Daughters of Sarah

Most of us remember Sarah best as the wizened wife of Abraham who laughed through her missing teeth when she discovered she was pregnant. But Scripture wants us to remember Sarah much differently—as the preeminent beauty of her day. She had the kind of "trophy" looks that could stop kings and pharoahs in their tracks. No other woman in Scripture is called "beautiful" as many times.

But as gorgeous women since Eve have discovered, beauty can attract a lot of snakes. In Sarah's case, her husband feared that powerful men would kill him to get to her. Twice Abraham asked Sarah to join him in a dangerous charade by pretending to be his sister. Sure enough, first the pharoah, then King Abimilech, claimed her—and let Abraham alone.

Her looks had saved his life, but at what cost? Imagine her relief when both times God revealed Abraham's deception before Sarah was sexually violated.

In the New Testament, all eyes are on Sarah again. Peter, in his marriage advice to Christian women, holds up Sarah as the model of a more lasting kind of beauty:

"Be submissive to your husbands so that, if any of them do not believe the word, they may be won over without words by the behavior of their wives . . . Your beauty should not come from outward adornment . . . It should be that of your inner self, the unfading beauty of a gentle and quiet spirit . . . For this is the way the holy women of the past who put their hope in God used to make themselves beautiful. They were submissive to their own husbands, like Sarah, who obeyed Abraham and called him her master. You are her daughters if you do what is right and do not give way to fear" (1 Peter 3:1-6).

A modern paraphrase of this passage might read: "Show respect and honor to your husband even if—no, especially if—he doesn't deserve it. He needs your help to see the right way to live and love. And when he sees your beautiful trust in God, he'll want that beauty for himself, too."

Inner beauty takes time and commitment. Ask any woman; it's easier to fix your hair than fix your attitude. Two key phrases in Peter's address stand out as memorable beauty tips for the inner life:

"Without words"—loving actions and attitudes are like just the right touch of perfume: They draw attention to the person, not the allure of the scent itself. How can you influence your husband with silent beauty today?

"Do not give way to fear"—Abraham did, when he tried to use Sarah's charms to rescue them. When we hang all our hopes for influence or appeal on cosmetics or body shape, we do too. But there's a timeless attraction that radiates from a trusting, assured, and hopeful woman. She looks more and more like Jesus.

Now there's a beauty that can shake up kings! And wake up husbands, too.

Jesus,

Do your beautiful work in my heart and spirit. May every word, deed, gesture, and look be a fragrance that will bring others to You. Amen.

 Do you know which of your inner qualities is most appreciated by your husband or wife? If not, ask. Then give this quality to God for His use in your marriage.

*The Lord said to Abram, "Leave your
country, your people and your father's household
and go the land I will show you. . . . So Abram
left, as the Lord had told him. . . . He took his
wife Sarai, his nephew Lot, all the possessions
they had accumulated and the people they had
acquired in Haran, and they set out for the land
of Canaan."*

—Genesis 12:1,4-5

3 The Journey of a Lifetime

Abraham's story is the first road movie of the Bible (after 11
chapters of special-effects masterpieces and action epics). No
sooner has Abraham pitched his tent in a roadside oasis than the
Lord says, "Time to move on." Abraham, already 75 years old,
leaves his birthplace near the Persian Gulf, travels to Haran (in
modern-day Syria), moves on to Canaan and Egypt, and then back
to Canaan. Even in Canaan he's a wanderer, always looking for
better pasture for his flocks. In a world of settlers, he's just passing
through.

All he takes with him are his wife and family, his possessions,
and God's solemn promise: "Go to the land I will show you. I will
bless you . . . and all peoples on earth will be blessed through you"
(Genesis 12:1-3).

In the book of Hebrews we read his one-paragraph biography:
"By faith Abraham, when called to go to a place he would later receive
as his inheritance, obeyed and went, even though he did not know
where he was going. By faith he made his home in the promised land
like a stranger in a foreign country..." (Hebrews 11:8-9).

Any husband or wife recognizes the language: *Leave . . . go . . .*

later...he did not know where he was going...stranger in a foreign country. When we knelt at the altar, we might have thought we were home safe. But that was only the first, "Yes, I'll go," and it was meant to be the first of many.

So where are we headed now?

God is leading us toward growth, toward healing, toward serving others. But the exact itinerary is not ours to know. The only directions we need are God's words in our ear: "Go...I will show you." We can move ahead through all life's unknowns with faith, not fear, because God knows the way. And He has chosen a route for us that is good (Job 23:10; Romans 8:28).

Once we let go of the "where?" questions, the next temptation is to ask the child's backseat question: "Are we there yet?" We can't seem to help ourselves. *"When* will we finally get to the place where we can leave the kids at home?" *"When* will we arrive at financial security?"

But Abraham and Sarah's story reminds us that, in so many ways, the journey *is* the destination. Marriage, like a marathon, isn't one long race; it's many short races run one after the other.

Can you identify some unknowns and insecurities in your marriage journey today? Finances? Health concerns? Work and career? Children?

With simple faith in the Lord, we must put aside any settler's assumptions that might be keeping our marriage stuck in one place. Then we can move forward, confident that God goes with us. And we take along this ancient pilgrim's blessing: "Blessed are those whose strength is in you, who have set their hearts on pilgrimage...They go from strength to strength" (Psalm 84:5-6).

Lord,

Forgive us for so often choosing safety and convenience, when we could have followed You forward in obedience. When our strength is gone, and we can hardly focus on the road ahead, lead us by Your love. We belong to You. Amen.

Talk about an "are we there yet?" question that is bothering one or both of you.

But Moses fled from Pharoah and went to live in Midian, where he sat down by a well. Now a priest of Midian had seven daughters, and they came to draw water and fill the troughs to water their father's flock. Some shepherds came along and drove them away, but Moses got up and came to their rescue and watered their flock.

—EXODUS 2:15-17

4 Set Apart for God

Any idea where this scene's headed? If you've read the pretty-girl-at-the-well stories of Isaac and Jacob, you'll remember. In ancient times, wells were the places to see and be seen. In Moses' and Jacob's romances, the flirting follows a similar pattern: Meet an attractive girl, do something to get her attention, then hope for an invitation home to meet Mom and Dad.

It worked for Moses. The girls ran home to tell their father about the Egyptian they'd met. In no time at all, "Moses agreed to stay with the man, who gave his daughter Zipporah to Moses in marriage" (Exodus 2:21).

But what a strange marriage! Moses is a Jew who looks and acts like an Egyptian (he's grown up in Pharoah's court). Zipporah is a pagan Midianite who's lived her whole life in the backside of beyond. Right from the start, you're asking the question, "Can this marriage be saved?"

Obviously young Zipporah had no idea what she was getting into when she married her handsome man from the city. Moses was on the run from a past crime (murder), his race (Jewish), and his real calling in life (to be a leader). He settled into life as a sheep-herder, trying to disappear from the public eye.

Many years passed before Moses set about to obey God. It was to be a decades-long sojourn that led through confrontations with Pharoah, plagues in Egypt, a miraculous escape through the Red Sea, the giving of the Law, and 40 years of desert survival.

But the first Zipporah heard of it was, "Honey, you'll never guess what happened at work today. There was this burning bush . . ."

The Bible tells us very little about Zipporah or her marriage. But God must have thought Moses needed a wife before launching him on his action-packed spiritual journey. The only recorded scene between the couple is almost bizarre. As they travel to Egypt so Moses can talk to Pharoah, the Bible says, "The LORD met Moses and was about to kill him" (Exodus 4:24). We don't know for certain what this means. Perhaps a sudden illness threatened his life.

Sensing that her husband's life is at stake, Zipporah intervenes. She realizes that they've neglected to circumcise their boy, and that this unfinished business is endangering them. So she performs the surgery herself, using a flint knife to mark the child as one of God's chosen people.

What can we learn from Moses and Zipporah? Maybe this: No matter what our differences, God wants to use both of us to lay claim to the future He has for us. With one flash of the flint, Moses and Zipporah decided who they wanted to be: chosen, set apart, and obedient. And then, together, they moved forward in faith to Moses' appointment with history.

Heavenly Father,
Bring my partner and me together in a radical commitment to walk in faith and obedience together. Only You can tie all the loose ends of our lives together and give us a future. Lead us there today. Amen.

How can you and your spouse make a radical choice for God in your marriage today? Can you say with Joshua, Moses' right hand man, "As for me and my house, we will serve the LORD"? (Joshua 24:15).

Go, assemble the elders of Israel and say to them, "The LORD, the God of your fathers . . . appeared to me and said: I have promised to bring you up out of your misery in Egypt into the land of the Canaanites . . . a land flowing with milk and honey."
—*God speaks to Moses* (EXODUS 3:16-17)

5 *Impossible Promises*

Abraham and Moses were each promised something by God that seemed impossible. And each responded with great, unwavering faith.

Well, not exactly. Yes, both Moses and Abraham were examples of faith. But they were also ordinary men beset by doubts and failings, especially when God singled them out to receive His personal, "impossible" promises. Moses, for example, argued with God about the hurdles ahead of him before his race ever began. Even after God gave him power to perform amazing signs, Moses whined, "O Lord, please send someone else" (Exodus 4:13).

Abraham's faith started out strong, and was "credited to him as righteousness." But what about 230 laps later, when Sarah still wasn't pregnant? When Sarah decided to help God out by giving Abraham her maid Hagar, Abraham agreed to jump the gun. The results were disastrous.

Corrie ten Boom once wrote, "Never be afraid to trust an unknown future to a known God." Where are you and your spouse today in regard to God's personal, impossible promises for you? Are you praying for:

- Peace, when all around you is pandemonium?

- Provision, when all you see is want and need?

- Healing, when illness or handicap hold you hostage?

- A child, the salvation of a spouse, meaningful work . . . ?

When you see outrageous obstacles looming in your path, ask: Is what I'm attempting impossible *enough* to bring God glory? No one could doubt God's involvement when Sarah became pregnant. And no one argued His power when the Red Sea parted. Faith sees obstacles and inadequacies as opportunities to let others see the truth about God.

Or is the challenge to your faith more like Abraham's? You're stuck in a waiting mode.

Hebrews 11:13 reminds us: "All these people were still living by faith when they died. They did not receive the things promised; they only saw them and welcomed them from a distance." In our spiritual lives and in our marriages, God looks for those whose vision is greater than just here and now. Faith keeps its eyes not on the clock or the track, but on the finish line.

Someone is waiting there for us: "Let us run with perseverance the race marked out for us . . . Let us fix our eyes on Jesus, the author and perfecter of our faith . . ." (Hebrews 12:1-2).

> *Faithful Lord,*
> *Help us to be Your faithful followers. We give You all our fears and failings. Give us Your strength and grace to endure. We want to make a lifetime of choices and actions that honor You. Amen.*

Love Talk

Write down an "impossible promise" that seems critical to your life together right now. Write: "The Lord is faithful to all His promises" after it, and tuck it in your Bible next to Psalm 145:13-19 or Hebrews 11–12.

CHAPTER THREE

Isaac & Rebekah

About Isaac

Name: Means "laughter"
Age at Marriage: 40
Appearance: Unknown
Personality: Peace-loving, a loner, trusting, loved his mother
Family Background: Only son of Abraham and Sarah, born in their old age
Place in History: Called "the child of promise"; second in line of Jewish patriarchs

About Rebekah

Name: Means "flattery"
Age at Marriage: Around 15–18
Appearance: Described as very beautiful
Personality: High-spirited, helpful, but portrayed as a schemer later in life
Family Background: Grew up in Mesopotamia; the grand-niece of Abraham
Place in History: She and Eve are the only Bible brides "personally selected" by God

Finding the Right One

Genesis 24

Lover's trivia question: The moment they look true love in the face, two pretty girls in the Bible run away. Who were they?

Answer:

1. Rebekah—She met Abraham's servant at the well and watered his camels. When he told her who he was and gave her gifts of jewelry (preengagement gifts), the Bible says "the girl ran and told her mother's household about these things" (Genesis 24:28).

2. Rachel—Soon after she laid eyes on Jacob, he threw his arms around her, kissed her, and told the startled girl he was her cousin. Rachel's first reaction? She "ran and told her father" (Genesis 29:12).

You'll find other parallels between Rebekah's and Rachel's stories, too:

- both girls are cousins from the same family (Laban's, in Aram)

- the men they will marry are from the same family (Abraham's, in Canaan)

- they each have a first encounter at a well

- and here's the best part—the love stories they embark
  on are among the favorites in all Scripture

As you'll find when you get to Jacob and Rachel's story, Jacob plays the suitor role like a modern romantic film hero. What sets Rebekah's story apart is that her husband-to-be doesn't court her at all. In fact, Isaac doesn't even enter the picture until a few days before the wedding. The story unfolds like this.

Abraham's wife, Sarah, has died. Their son, Isaac, whom they'd conceived when they were already old, is now in middle age himself and unmarried. But he seems lost in grief over the death of his mother.

Abraham decides it's time to act. He calls his chief servant, Eliezer, and tells him to go back to the country of Abraham's forebears and find his son a wife. The local heathen girls won't do for his Isaac. After all, Isaac is the "child of promise"—through him God has promised to make a great nation.

When Eliezer mumbles something about, "Well, what if the girl I pick doesn't want to come back with me?" Abraham makes an astounding promise. God will be the matchmaker. His angel will go ahead of Eliezer and lead him to the right girl.

So Eliezer leaves for Paddan Aram, 500 hundred miles away, with a caravan full of gifts. Finally, at the end of a hot day of travel, he arrives. He is resting at an oasis in the cool of the evening when he sees a girl approaching. Wasting no time, he prays, "May it be that when I say to a girl, 'Please let down your jar that I may have a drink,' and she says, 'Drink, and I'll water your camels, too'—let her be the one . . ." (Genesis 24:14).

When Rebekah's response matches the servant's prayer exactly, he knows the angel is there at the oasis with them. And the lovely girl working away to water ten thirsty camels must be the one for Isaac.

That evening over dinner, the match is confirmed when Laban, Rebekah's father, agrees. "This is from the Lord," he exclaims. When he asks Rebekah how soon she'll be ready to leave, she doesn't hesitate. "Let's go now," she says.

The next day, after the servant showers Rebekah's family with gifts of gold, jewelry, and clothing, the caravan heads for home. Rebekah rides off with them to the southwest, perched on her camel.

As far as we know, Rebekah never saw her family again.

Talk about guts. Suddenly we see that girl racing away from the well toward her mother in a new light. She wasn't scared. She was excited, running *toward* a future she wanted.

Maybe one reason we resonate with this story is that it's a family drama that combines so many of the elements about meeting and mating that stir us:

- A lonely bachelor
- A faithful, understanding father
- A resourceful family friend
- One obstacle after another
- An angel
- An adventurous young girl
- A journey toward love of many miles and many unknowns

If the TV show *Touched by an Angel* were to pick one Bible story for today's viewers, this would be it: an interesting couple destined for one another but with no chance of meeting—then an angel shows up.

In the meditations that follow, we'll start with the charming "made in heaven" aspect of this story. But we'll go further. We'll ask, for example: If God matched the pair, why? What can we learn about finding and keeping the right marriage partner? About the role of parents? About leaving families behind? About protecting our marriage from split loyalties?

We might not quite identify with young Rebekah's risky choice, but we do know this: Every marriage requires a journey into the unknown. Even after a lengthy courtship, we can still sense we're riding off with a stranger. But Isaac and Rebekah's story reassures us that if we seek God's best and bring a heart full of courage, it can be the best journey of our life.

Then he (the servant) prayed, "O Lord, God of my master Abraham, give me success today. . . . May it be that when I say to a girl, 'Please let down your jar that I may have a drink,' and she says, 'Drink, and I'll water your camels too'—let her be the one you have chosen for our servant Isaac."

—GENESIS 24:12-14

The Matchmaker from Heaven

In many ways, Isaac and Rebekah's marriage reads like a fairy tale. One day Rebekah wakes up and discovers that the glass slipper fits. Her kind gesture to a stranger has suddenly transformed her from a watering girl into the bride-to-be for a rich, important man. Now it's time to run off and marry him.

But there's a catch. She has to travel hundreds of miles by camel just to meet him.

Isaac and Rebekah's love story is full of such intriguing twists. God (through an angel) plays matchmaker on the father's behalf, while a servant does the courting. Throughout the story, we're reminded that it is God who is maneuvering behind the scenes. He has the storyline firmly in his grip—the characters just have to hang on and trust Him.

Isaac and Rebekah had to put extraordinary faith in God's matchmaking abilities. We can imagine their very human hesitations: What if the servant returns with a woman only a mother could love? What if Isaac turns out to be as bad-tempered as a Canaanite mule?

Their story reminds us to be brave for love, and to trust the Matchmaker of heaven with our heart's desires. No one knows better than God whom we should marry—and that's no fairy tale.

In fact, it's no coincidence that although not a single word is recorded between the lovers in this story, the word *love* is used romantically here for the first time in the Bible—"So she became his wife, and he *loved* her" (Genesis 24:67). It's as if God is saying, "See, I know what I'm doing!"

God may not send a visible angel to help us, but he cares infinitely about how our love story turns out. He is ready right now to work in surprising ways on our behalf—whether we're just starting out or already well into our marriage journey. We should ask Him earnestly for guidance, and we should listen carefully to His reply—through family, His promises, and His Spirit in our heart.

After all, every story of lifelong devotion really belongs to Him—"If we love one another, God lives in us and his love is made complete in us" (1 John 4:12). And if Isaac and Rebekah could talk to us today, they might lean down from their camels long enough to say: *"The Matchmaker in heaven knows your heart— and your future. Trust Him with your dreams, even if the journey is long."*

> Matchmaker in Heaven,
> How good it is to know that You desire to be intimately involved in our decisions about love and marriage. Lord, You see across the miles and the years. We surrender our dreams to You. Bring them back with Your blessings a hundred times better than we could ever imagine. Because You are just that kind of God. In Jesus' name we pray. Amen.

What kind of strange twists do you and your spouse find in the story of your relationship? What do you think God might have been trying to teach you through these?

> *"The LORD has blessed my master abundantly, and he has become wealthy. He has given him sheep and cattle, silver and gold, menservants and maidservants, and camels and donkeys. My master's wife Sarah has borne him a son in her old age, and he has given him everything he owns."*
>
> —GENESIS 24:35-36

2 Is This the Right One?

When Eliezer spoke these words to Rebekah's family, he was in essence making his "pitch" for Rebekah's hand in marriage to Isaac. For Hebrew parents, finding a mate for their children constituted important family business. A daughter was an asset that would go to another family (how much would they pay for her?); a son would bring assets to his own family (how well could he do?).

This approach might seem unfeeling, even wrong to us. Many today don't take concerns about family or spiritual backgrounds too seriously. If money matters, we don't like to talk about it. Instead, we want to look good together, to be "meant for each other" (whatever that means). We want sparks, sweet talk about "our song," a smashing wedding.

And parents? Their job is to foot the bill.

But is our modern approach really better? Our version of wedded bliss tends to fade early—just look at the divorce statistics, even for Christians. Maybe one reason is that we focus so much on feelings—as if they're all we need.

You might think Rebekah's story tells us there's nothing wrong with marrying on impulse, or that God will provide instantaneous revelation of "the right one" for us. But God is not talking about magic here. If you look past the part about the angel, you'll find a lot of good everyday common sense for finding a Christian mate:

- Shared values and family background—Abraham clearly wanted Isaac's wife to share the same family background: "Go to my father's family and to my own clan, and get a wife for my son" (verse 38).

- Spiritual compatibility—Abraham insisted that Isaac marry a believer: "You must not get a wife for my son from the daughters of the Canaanites" (verse 37). It was worth a thousand-mile trip to make this happen.

- Character—The servant's on-the-spot test at the well revealed his criteria for a good spouse: She would have to care about the needs of others, be helpful, hard-working, and selfless—with plenty of spunk (verses 43-44).

- Parental blessing—The servant consulted with Rebekah's parents. Their reaction helped him know whether or not the plan was of the Lord (verse 50).

- Enthusiasm—Eliezer's question to Abraham, "What if she won't come back with me?" implies that the bride's feelings would matter. And Rebekah's eagerness to leave for Canaan was the response he had hoped for (verses 57-58).

The big idea in this love story is simple, powerful, and still true: If we seek God's best in our decisions, He'll guide us in practical ways every step of the way.

> *Lord,*
> *Thank You that when it comes to the small and large decisions of love, marriage, and life, You don't leave us in the dark. You promise to lead us along unfamiliar paths and turn our darkness into light (Isaiah 42:16). Thank You, too, for friends and family who can help us at these critical times. Bless every choice we make today, and by Your angels, protect and direct us. Amen.*

Can you think of times when God brought you wisdom to make difficult choices? In areas where you are seeking His leading now, how can you watch for His presence and His promptings?

He went out to the field one evening to medi-
tate, and as he looked up, he saw camels ap-
proaching. Rebekah also looked up and saw
Isaac. She got down from her camel and asked
the servant, "Who is that man in the field
coming to meet us?"
—GENESIS 24:63-65

3 Marriage Maker

Imagine how Rebekah felt when Eliezer answered, "He is my master." *So this was the one!* At last she was about to meet the mystery man about whom she'd been plying the servant with questions for miles and miles. Would she love him? Would he be taken with her?

We're told that Isaac's immediate reaction to Rebekah was positive. We are told that he loved her. But we aren't told about her feelings. Maybe she had to grow into love. Maybe she sometimes lay in bed at night, missing her far-away home, and wondering, "Was I crazy to say yes?"

As in any marriage, surely Rebekah wasn't always *exactly* what Isaac wanted either. If he'd made a list back then of the qualities he was looking for in a spouse—a popular and potentially helpful practice among Christian singles today—he probably would have listed near the top: "She will give me many sons." Yet Rebekah was barren for the first 20 years of their marriage.

In fact, Genesis reveals that Isaac and Rebekah went on to have many serious struggles in their marriage, mostly over their children. But this didn't mean they were *wrong* for each other, or that God made a mistake. It simply reminds us that even a marriage "made in heaven" must be lived out day-by-day on earth—with and in spite of our human shortcomings.

Ultimately, this story is not just about God's matchmaking abilities. It is also about God's *marriage-making* abilities. No matter how difficult our relationship, when we made a covenant of marriage with God and our mate, God took it to heart. There is no record in the Bible of God saying, "Whoops! Can't work with *that* marriage!"

Whether we've been married two months or 20 years, if we have committed to our mate, and said, "Yes, I will," God will give us the courage we need to say yes to that person every day.

Like us, Isaac and Rebekah couldn't really know what God was accomplishing through their meeting and marriage. In their case, it was building the foundations of the Jewish nation. The God who brought them together so dramatically never once abandoned them in the marriage that followed.

What could God be accomplishing in your marriage today? When you say yes to Him, you gain the strength to work through whatever disappointments come your way.

> *Marriage Maker in Heaven,*
> *Thank You that no matter what happens now, no matter how we might have failed in the past—You are a redeemer and restorer of our marriage. Help us to choose each other over and over again, just as Your mercies toward us are new every morning (Lamentations 3:22,23). We want to build a marriage together that brings You honor and pleasure. Amen.*

 Love Talk

Have you ever wondered whether you made the wrong choice in a mate? What needs or disappointments were behind your feelings? What assures you that God, your marriage-maker, has chosen each of you for the other?

4 "I Will Go"

"I will go," said Rebekah. Three words that would change her life forever. Kind of like saying, "I do."

When Rebekah agreed to leave her family and travel with this stranger back to Canaan, she experienced what it meant to "leave" her mother and father in the most literal sense. And the parents who watched her disappear in the cloud of dust kicked up by her camels would never again lay eyes on their daughter, much less attend her wedding!

Today we often leave home for college or our own apartment long before we're married. But the principle expressed in Genesis, "a man shall leave his father and his mother . . ." is not just talking about a physical leaving, but an emotional parting as well.

This means that we give up our dependency—financial, emotional, and social—on our parents and create a new bond with each other built upon loyalty, time, and attention. We take what we have learned from one home and we use it to create another.

God knew that if we didn't leave our first home completely, we would be hindered by split loyalties as we tried to build a second one. And so, part of every marriage is saying as Rebekah

65

did, "I will go. I will leave my parents behind and make a journey toward my lifelong partner. Ready the camels!"

Of course, sometimes this "leaving" is harder than it sounds. Elizabeth Barrett Browning once wrote, "If I leave all for thee, wilt thou exchange and be all to me?" A similar refrain must have echoed in Rebekah's heart as she traveled away from the familiar toward the strange.

When Isaac took Rebekah into his mother's tent, he too was "leaving" his parents. Some scholars speculate that it was because of Isaac's strong attachment to his mother that Abraham waited so long—until Isaac was 40—to see his "promised child" married. When Isaac brought Rebekah into his mother's tent and found comfort in her, he was allowing her to occupy that treasured place in his heart and home which formerly belonged to his mother.

There are some of us, however, for whom it's not affection that ties us to a parent, but rather unresolved conflict or fear or immaturity. For those who have been hurt in childhood relationships, bitterness and unforgiveness can continue to tie us emotionally to our parents in ways that can interfere with our marital unity.

When we are truly able to leave our mother and father—emotionally as well as physically—we can form a bond with our spouse that is even stronger. As Mike Mason writes in *Mystery of Marriage*, "To be married is to find in a total stranger a near and long lost relative, a true-blood relative even closer than father or mother."

> Lord of Married Lovers,
>   Please reveal to us if there are any ways that I or my spouse still haven't "left home." We want to be able to truly cleave to one another—and love our parents as well—without being tripped up by loyalty conflicts, old

hurts, or unhealthy dependencies on Mom or Dad.
Thank You for giving us a mate who has the potential to
be as close as any relative. Amen.

 What keeps you tied in an unhealthy way to one parent or another (or if you've been previously married, to a former spouse)?

The boys grew up, and Esau became a skillful hunter, a man of the open country, while Jacob was a quiet man, staying among the tents. Isaac, who had a taste for wild game, loved Esau, but Rebekah loved Jacob.
—GENESIS 25:27-28

The Most
5 Important One

At first glance, Isaac and Rebekah's favoritism with their sons sounds pretty harmless—and it probably felt that way to the couple at the time. Isaac probably would have shrugged it off and said, "Esau and I both enjoy the outdoors. So what?" And Rebekah probably reasoned it couldn't be wrong to spend so much time having heart-to-heart talks with Jacob.

Neither may have realized that one day these split loyalties would lead to a deep split—involving treachery, deceit, and betrayal—in their marriage.

As Isaac, aged, blind, and near death, prepared to bestow his blessing on Esau (a legally binding oath usually given to the first-born son) Rebekah prepared to trick her husband. By helping Jacob pose as his brother Esau, she saw to it that Isaac's blessing was mistakenly and irretrievably bestowed on her favorite son.

What led Rebekah to do such a thing?

Perhaps Rebekah's first mistake was that she lacked faith in God's timing and ways. God had already told Rebekah when she was pregnant that "the older will serve the younger" (Genesis 25:24) But so far as Rebekah could see—which wasn't very far—this wasn't happening. Rebekah needed to call on the kind of courage and faith that had initially brought her and Jacob together all those years ago. But instead, Rebekah took it upon herself to try to force God's hand.

Rebekah's second mistake stemmed from something good in itself—her deep devotion to her son. In and of itself, this wasn't bad. But as she and Isaac played favorites with their children over the years, something else was also happening. Their loyalties to their kids became more important than their loyalty to each other. And the moment Rebekah decided to trick her husband, she put her love for Jacob ahead of her love for Isaac and her marriage.

This part of Isaac and Rebekah's story reminds us of a very basic but easily missed marriage principle: *No person on earth should become more important to us than our spouse.* In every marriage, other people—important people—vie for our affections, attentions, and loyalties. In some cases it is our kids. Other times our loyalty to parents can get in the way or our devotion to a career can gradually take first place in our hearts.

"Forsaking all others" means more than just sexual fidelity. Finding the "right one" is just the start. Keeping that person as the *most important one* is how we will guard our marriage and go the distance together.

> Lord,
>   How easily my faith in how You work behind the scenes fades as I get older. Keep me bold for love! Save me from letting weakness or convenience or favoritism drive a wedge between my spouse and me today. You are at work, Lord—and I trust You! Amen.

 Love Talk | Do you feel replaced by another loyalty? How could reclaiming shared goals help resolve this?

CHAPTER FOUR

Jacob, Rachel, Leah

About Jacob

Name: Means "heel-grabber" (later changed to Israel, "prince")
Personality: Resourceful, scheming, and hard-working, but also deeply spiritual and emotionally vulnerable
Place in History: The most colorful Jewish patriarch; father of the 12 tribes of Israel

About Rachel

Name: Means "lamb"
Appearance: "Lovely in form and feature"
Personality: Bright, determined, and competitive
Place in History: Favored second wife of Jacob; mother of Benjamin and Joseph

About Leah

Name: Means "cow"
Age at Marriage: Around 22
Appearance: Traditionally thought to be very plain, with sensitive eyes or poor vision
Personality: Responsible, kind, persevering
Place in History: Unloved first wife of Jacob; mother of six sons, including Levi and Judah, whose descendants were especially important in Israel's history

When Love Is Hard Work

Genesis 29

Pick up the Old Testament Yearbook, Class of 1900 (B.C.), and under a photo of a sharply featured young man with piercing eyes you read—"Jacob, son of Isaac of Beersheba. Member: Young Entreprenuers of Canaan, Wrestling Team, and Debate Club. Favorite Quote: 'Start first, finish strong, and get away fast.' Voted 'Most Likely to Succeed,' and 'Most Likely to Cheat Your Father.'"

A girl has written, "Hey, mama's boy!" beside the picture.

Another classmate has scrawled, "Do we hafta be on the same page?" That leads your eye to the next photo. It's of a brawny outdoor type with a thick head of hair and too many teeth for his lopsided grin. The entry reads: "Esau, son of Isaac of Beersheba . . ."

Now you've met one of the Bible's most fascinating characters (along with his older twin brother). As predicted by classmates, Jacob goes on to become a notorious schemer and dreamer. But he develops a deeper side, too—emotional, caring, intelligent, and spiritually motivated. And as you might expect, Jacob's experience in marriage was just as full of surprises as his yearbook profile might suggest.

Jacob was the third in line of Israel's founding fathers—after Isaac, his father, and Abraham, his grandfather. Through Abraham came God's promise to make his descendants as numerous as the stars and to bless the whole world through them (Genesis 22:17-18). But Jacob didn't want to leave anything to chance. First, he smooth-talked Esau out of the family birthright. Then, with the help of his mother Rebekah, he deceived his father, Isaac, into bestowing the family blessing on him, rather than his brother.

Cheating this close to home put him on the run (probably right after that yearbook photo session). With Esau breathing murder threats, Jacob fled to Paddan Aram, where his mother's family lived. But before he had even unpacked his camel, he was captured by love.

Her name was Rachel. She was a young beauty he met at a well, who turned out to be his cousin. When her father, Laban, invited Jacob to work for him, Jacob made a counter offer: "I'll work for you seven years in return for your younger daughter Rachel" (Genesis 29:18).

This is where Jacob's tangled marriage story begins. You could say that Jacob's and Rachel's story is about the gift of love—and the yearly payment plan that follows. Rachel's father, Laban, agreed to give her hand in marriage in exchange for seven years of hard labor. We're told, "So Jacob served seven years to get Rachel, but they seemed like only a few days to him because of his love for her" (Genesis 29:20).

Through seven years of sweat and dirt, flies and ticks, stinking goats, and stubborn sheep, summer heat and winter cold, Jacob never wavered. But when Jacob's time to marry Rachel finally arrived, Laban tricked him. On Jacob's wedding night, Laban slipped Rachel's older sister, Leah, into the bridal chamber instead. Jacob awoke the next morning to the shock of his life.

According to one story in Jewish folklore, Jacob rebukes Leah: "O thou deceiver, daughter of a deceiver, why did you answer me when I called Rachel's name?"

To which Leah replies: "Is there a teacher without a pupil? I learned from your example. Did you not answer your father when he called Esau?"

Laban explained to an outraged Jacob that it was against custom to marry off the younger daughter before the elder. Then he told his new son-in-law he could have Rachel too, if he was willing to work another seven years. When Jacob's anger subsided, he made the only choice his heart would allow. After the week-long wedding celebration for Leah was done, Jacob took Rachel as his second wife—and started over on another payment plan.

The focus of the story then shifts to the two sisters (each as different from the other as Jacob was from his twin, Esau). Leah and Rachel sink into a bitter rivalry over Jacob's attentions. Beautiful Rachel wins Jacob's desire for her (he hardly notices plain Leah), but fertile Leah satisfies Jacob's desire for sons (Rachel can't get pregnant).

The "baby wars" keep Jacob's household in a continual uproar. But they have one important payoff—by the time Jacob returns to Canaan, he is the father of 12 sons and at least one daughter. In time the sons become the heads of clans, and eventually, of the 12 twelve tribes of Israel.

What do we find in the stress-filled love story of Jacob, Leah, and Rachel that can bring hope to our own?

Plenty. The marriage of these three fascinating people is rich with lessons on maintaining a loving relationship when nothing comes quickly or easily. We'll explore themes like waiting, jealousy, feeling uncherished, and how to finally find contentment.

Jacob's life, his marriages, and his fathering were all pretty untidy by any standard (some of us can relate). But for all his wrestling to get what he wants out of life, he also keeps striving to receive God's blessings (see Genesis 31:22-32). And God rewards him time and again by arriving on the scene with His promise: "I will bless you! Good things are on the way!"

In our marriages, God has something good in mind, too. Our character traits and mistakes—past and present—don't change that; our unpromising yearbook entries don't either. We can count on the Lord of love to bless us—and others through us—if we reach every day for His blessing with all our hearts.

So Jacob served seven years to get Rachel,
but they seemed like only a few days to him
because of his love for her.

1 Worth the Wait

Jacob was the first man in the Bible to prove Albert Einstein's theory of relativity. This theory, as you know, says that time is relative to how fast you're moving. Here's Jacob's journey through time.

Jacob had always been a young man in a hurry. He'd already proved that he didn't like standing in line behind his brother Esau to get what he wanted (Genesis 25:29-34; 27:1-46). Then, as soon as he arrived in Paddan Aram, he fell for Rachel and a month later proposed marriage. Cash-poor, Jacob rashly offered to work seven years to pay for his bride. What's seven years when you're in love? *Tick, tick, tick. . . .* Why, it's mere seconds. The Bible says the years passed by in a flash—"they seemed like only a few days to him."

But then, time began to slow down.

First there was the problem of Rachel's barrenness. Rachel waited, through seven childbirths by her sister Leah plus two by Leah's maid. And Jacob waited with her (Genesis 29:31–30:21), wondering whether God would ever answer their prayers and relieve his dear Rachel of her agony. The months crawled by.

Then there was Laban, his scheming father-in-law. He always had yet one more airtight reason for Jacob and his growing family to stay in Paddan Aram instead of leaving for home (Genesis 30:25-31:55). Would they ever earn back their freedom? The years seemed to stretch on forever.

And what about the wrestling match in the dark? An angel got Jacob in a hammer lock and "wrestled with him till daybreak" (Genesis 32:24). How long is a night when it seems like God Himself is tearing apart your tendons? *Tick, tick, tick, tick. . . .*Why, it's long enough to break you of proud self-sufficiency for the rest of your life.

Time is relative in our marriages, too. We wait with great anticipation for the wedding day—the consummation of years of hoping, planning, and dreaming. We wait excitedly for the birth of children, for a first house, for a family vacation. And time flies.

But sometimes the waiting is long and heart-wrenching. We hold on through illness or disability, persevere through the rebellion of a wayward child or spouse, push on through financial hardship or spiritual testing. At such times, life inches along and bailing out can look very appealing.

How do we wait well? We can accept every "time zone" of life as being from God's loving hand. He's always at work for our good (Romans 8:28). We can tell Him today, "I trust in you, O LORD; I say, 'You are my God.' My times are in your hands . . ." (Psalm 31:14-15). Then, we are free to follow Paul's time-tested advice: "Be joyful in hope *(good times)*, patient in affliction *(bad times)*, faithful in prayer *(all times)*" (Romans 12:12).

Time moves at its own pace and our perception of it keeps changing. But God remains constant. We can wait on Him with confidence (Psalm 27:13,14). And, through prayer, we can wait *with* Him in strength and peace.

Lord,

Waiting is hard, and my human nature would rather skip it altogether. But You are the Lord of time. Use our seasons of waiting to accomplish Your purposes in our marriage. And bless us with a powerful sense of Your presence with us today. Amen.

Love Talk | What are you waiting for? What good things are happening in the meantime? How can you help each other wait in hope?

*Then Jacob said to Laban, "Give me my wife.
My time is completed, and I want to lie with
her." But when evening came, he took his
daughter Leah and gave her to Jacob, and Jacob
lay with her . . . When morning came, there
was Leah!*

—GENESIS 29:21,23,25

2 *Please Love Me*

With just six words—"When morning came, there was
Leah!"—the Bible conjures up a scene that sets the imagination
spinning. Jacob wakes up to the first morning of married life
with a sleepy smile on his lips, rolls over to kiss his bride, and . . .
"Yikes! What is Leah doing in my bed?!"

Our first reaction is to pity Jacob. But what about Leah?
Her father's callousness has landed her in a marriage where
she isn't wanted. Next to darling Rachel, Leah is Plain Jane.
Permanent second fiddle. Background music for someone else's
love affair . . .

We don't know if Leah starts out loving Jacob, but we do know
this—once married, every decision she makes in her baby war
with Rachel (Genesis 29-30) is calculated to win her husband's
affection.

We catch a glimpse of Leah's desperation at the birth of her
first son. She says, "The Lord has seen my misery. Surely my
husband will love me now" (Genesis 29:32). But each new baby
is only another milestone in her lonely journey. Her attempts to
win Jacob's heart are doomed to fail.

Maybe you, like Leah, feel unloved. Your situation may not be dramatic or obvious, but you feel second-rate, unattractive, almost invisible to the one who promised to cherish you always.

You're not alone. In a recent marriage survey, one young mom told *Christian Parenting Today* magazine: "I'm beginning to despise my husband's call to the ministry. He's never home. The girls and I hardly exist for him except on Sundays when he wants us all dolled up." And a husband wrote, "Since our third child arrived, my wife barely notices me. Cheri has what she wants now. My job is to bring home the paychecks."

This issue resists easy answers, often because two spouses want or need different things from the same marriage. Leah certainly couldn't become Rachel. But in Leah's story, we find hope. God didn't rescue her from her loveless marriage, but through the long years, He never took His eyes off her. Buried in her story, we find comments like, "When the Lord saw that Leah was not loved, he opened her womb . . ." (Genesis 29:31), and, "God listened to Leah . . ." (30:17).

You see, another Lover was on the scene of this crazy, three-sided marriage. While Jacob was pursuing Rachel, God was pursuing and caring for Leah. As it turned out, Leah, not Rachel, played the critical role in giving birth to the twelve sons who would become the tribes of Israel.

Scholars note, too, that when Jacob died, he chose to be buried next to Leah, not Rachel. Perhaps in later life, Leah's years of work bloomed into love after all. Those in lonely marriages have often found comfort in Isaiah's reminder to Israel: "For your Maker is your husband—the Lord Almighty is his name. . . . The Lord will call you back as if you were a wife deserted and distressed in spirit—a wife who married young, only to be rejected . . . with deep compassion I will bring you back" (Isaiah 54:5-7).

In God's heart, we're always first.

Loving God,

Thank You for Your unfailing love. I praise You that no matter what my spouse does, says, or thinks—You will always be here for me. Show us how to truly cherish each other today. In Jesus' name. Amen.

Love Talk | Do you know someone who feels unloved in marriage? Pray for that person today, and ask God to show you a practical way to be a comfort to them (2 Corinthians 1:3-7).

Laban replied, "It is not our custom here to give the younger daughter in marriage before the older one. Finish this daughter's bridal week; then we will give you the younger one also, in return for another seven years of work."
—Genesis 29:26-27

3 *When the Price Doubles*

Jacob, the Bible's most famous hustler, had already proved that he knew how to manipulate the circumstances to get his way. But love—love he had to work for. And just when he thought he knew what love would cost him, the price doubled.

We never know when—or even how many times a day—we'll be required to put our personal price tag on love. What husband or wife hasn't reached a point in their marriage when the price of commitment suddenly seemed to double? Everything becomes much harder than we could possibly have imagined.

How much is marriage worth, anyway? One insight we might draw from Jacob's life would be this: *Marriage is worth a lot more than we can pay.*

But this might be just what God has in mind. "If it weren't hard, impossibly hard, why would there be any need for powerful and demanding marriage vows?" writes Neil Clark Warren in *Finding the Love of Your Life.* "We could just ask people to repeat something like this:

"I, James, take you, Susan, to be my wife. I promise to love you whenever possible. When you are worthy of it, I will honor you. When I want something from you and you give it to me, I will cherish you. If everything goes well between us, our relationship will continue. From my point of view it will mostly depend upon you, and I wish you nothing but the best."

This kind of marital "limited warranty" sounds just trendy enough to be possible: a business deal posing as a marriage. Both parties enjoy the benefits or call it quits. Warren goes on to say, "After years of working with couples struggling to stay together, I have concluded marriage is almost never a good 'business deal.' It is folly to think that you can ever know enough about another person to be assured that marriage will be a good deal for the next 40, 50, 60 years. . . . If you continually examine how beneficial and rewarding the relationship is for you, you'll be disappointed time after time."

If Jacob had measured his marriage in such terms, he probably would have bailed out. But the miracle of love had already changed him. When Jacob chose to pay twice for Rachel, for the very first time he looked away from getting what he deserved and reached toward what he could offer. Through seven years of opportunity for second thoughts, Jacob never wavered. This was surprising new behavior for the man with a reputation back home for cheating his way to success.

How much *is* love worth, anyway? Solomon would tell us, "If one were to give all the wealth of his house for love, it would be utterly scorned" (Song of Songs 8:7). And Jacob wouldn't hesitate to agree. He'd peer into our eyes and say, "If you want to know what true love is worth, set the highest price possible—then go twice as far."

Heavenly Father,

I thank You today for the priceless gift of my marriage. Show me how to treasure it, how to invest in it day after day. Especially help me during those times when it feels like our relationship is costing me—in terms of effort, or commitment—more than I want to pay. I want to become more and more like You, who paid the greatest price of all by sending Your Son to die for us. Amen.

 Find a creative way to tell your spouse what he or she is worth to you today.

When Rachel saw that she was not bearing Jacob any children, she became jealous of her sister . . .

—GENESIS 30:1

But she [Leah] said to her [Rachel], "Wasn't it enough that you took away my husband? Will you take my son's mandrakes too?"

—GENESIS 30:15

4 Seeing Green

It's the stuff of daytime talk shows: two sisters fighting over one man; weapon of choice—babies. Although Rachel is the wife Jacob loves, Leah is the wife who keeps getting pregnant. This makes Rachel green with jealousy.

When the baby tally reaches Leah—4, Rachel—still 0, Rachel screams at her husband, "Give me children, or I'll die!" (Genesis 30:1).

Jacob snaps back, "Am I in the place of God, who has kept you from having children?" (verse 2).

Then Rachel does what we might have done in a jealous fit— she takes matters into her own hands. She sends her servant Bilhah to Jacob in her place. Soon Leah does the same with her maid, Zilpah. Both maids begin adding babies to Jacob's fold on behalf of their mistresses. In no time at all, the score stands at 11 bawling babies, three nursing mothers, two feuding wives (one still infertile), and one sleepless husband. No one is living happily ever after.

On the one hand, we understand Rachel's fierce desires. After all, from her wedding night on, she had to share her husband with an intruder—and this was after waiting seven years for the marriage. And to be infertile was even more traumatizing in her day than it is now. But the way Rachel handled her pain caused bitterness and misery for everyone. When she traded Leah a night with Jacob for a fertility potion, her plan backfired (guess who got pregnant again?).

Jealousy seems to come into our marriages stuck to the bottom of our rented wedding shoes. All of us feel painful twinges of fear and insecurity now and then. Such jealousy can be healthy when it puts us on guard to protect our love from rival forces. But when we act out of the dark side of jealousy—our own fear, anger, and self-concern—we set up patterns that push away the mate we wanted to draw closer.

At the very least, unchecked jealousy in marriage destroys oneness and intimacy. "Anger is cruel and fury overwhelming, but who can stand before jealousy?" wrote Solomon (Proverbs 27:4). And how many stories on the 10 o'clock news involve stalking, murderous ex-lovers, and other crimes of jealousy? Paul lists jealousy (along with witchcraft, drunkenness, and sexual immorality) as behavior that excludes a person from the kingdom of God.

Is there hope for keeping that green-eyed monster out of our marriage? Yes. Paul goes on to say, "But the fruit of the Spirit is love, joy, peace, patience, kindness, goodness, faithfulness, gentleness and self control. . . . Those who belong to Christ Jesus have crucified the sinful nature with its passions and desires. Since we live by the Spirit, let us keep in step with the Spirit" (Galatians 5:22-25).

Through God's Spirit at work in us, we can post a winning score for our marriage: green-eyed monster—0, love—10 and climbing.

Lord,

Help us to never give each other reasons for jealousy. Be Lord of our relationship, exposing our sinful tendencies to Your light. We desire to have a marriage that honors You. By Your power, help us cultivate the kind of perfect love that casts out all fear. Amen.

Describe an instance of healthy protectiveness in your relationship, as well as an instance of destructive jealousy. Set up boundaries that you can agree upon together. Decide how you'll handle doubts or insecurities.

> *So Jacob sent word to Rachel and Leah to come out to the fields where his flocks were. He said to them, "I see that your father's attitude toward me is not what it was before, but the God of my father has been with me. You know that I've worked for your father with all my strength, yet your father has cheated me by changing my wages ten times. However, God has not allowed him to harm me."*
>
> —Genesis 39:4-8

5 *The Work of Peace*

At last the "baby wars" seem to be over. Jacob is now a father of 12 and a wealthy man. One day when he's out in the fields surrounded by sheep, he sends a message to his two wives. "Come out to the fields," he tells them. "We have to talk."

This is probably as close to a family meeting as this threesome has ever had. Jacob stands ready under a blue sky as Leah and Rachel draw close. Something important is about to happen. Jacob begins by reviewing his years of labor for their father. Then he tells them that God has appeared to him in a dream and told him to return to his native land at once.

Flocks bleat nearby, breezes ruffle their hair, and the sisters listen patiently. Now Jacob's unspoken question hangs in the air. Will they leave their father and come with him? Does he have their support?

For once, Rachel and Leah agree. Without hesitation they answer, "Surely all the wealth that God took away from our father belongs to us and our children. So do whatever God has told you" (Genesis 31:16).

In this one brief exchange, the Bible interrupts this tumultuous saga of love and pain with a picture of family harmony: a husband, two sisters, a marriage. And for the first time since the young, impulsive Jacob saw Rachel at the well and fell in love, we sense that everything is going to be okay.

After years of striving—against his brother, against his father-in-law, even against God, Jacob has turned a corner. He is now striving to make things right—first, within his own marriage; then (clumsily) with his father-in-law (Genesis 31:45-55); and at the end of the journey they're about to begin, with his estranged brother, Esau (32:1-33:20). By the time Jacob is back in Canaan, living at Bethel ("house of God") he is finally a man at peace.

A new kind of "striving"—for peace and harmony—had become the key to Jacob's maturity. This kind of striving is an important quality of any mature love affair. So many of us convince ourselves we're working hard at our relationship when instead we're really working hard at changing our circumstances or our spouses. When we strive stubbornly for what we want, we're nearly always striving *against* each other and our marriage. What a waste of "the work of love"!

It took Paul many years before he could finally say, "I have learned the secret of being content" (Philippians 4:12). Imagine the power of healing and encouragement in that statement if you could turn to your partner today and say, "Honey, things don't have to be going great for me to be content. And I don't need to change a thing about you. I just love you."

Today, God invites us out into the quiet fields with Jacob, Leah, and Rachel. We can let go of our frantic schemes—they never added up to much anyway. Our "marriage work" today is simply to receive the gift of peace that Christ offers.

Heavenly Father,
Forgive me for working on the wrong things in my
marriage. Help me today to trust You and love my mate
without reservation. Help me not to punish my relation-
ship because of my misguided frustrations. Help me
reach for Your gift of peace today. Amen.

Paul wrote, "Let the peace of Christ rule in your hearts since as members of one body you were called to peace. And be thankful" (Colossians 3:15). What word or action could help peace "rule" in your marriage today?

CHAPTER FIVE

Samson & Delilah

About Samson

Name: Means "sun" or "brightness"
Age at Marriage: About 40
Appearance: Long hair worn in 7 braids; bulky, muscular form
Personality: Charming, brave, rebellious, vengeful, a womanizer
Family Background: Father was Manoah from the tribe of Dan
Place in History: The last of the judges, Samson led Israel for 20 years

About Delilah

Name: Means "dainty one"
Age: Around 20
Appearance: Traditionally thought to be very beautiful, probably petite
Personality: Greedy, selfish, smart, manipulative, seductive
Family Background: A Philistine from the Valley of Sorek
Place in History: Famous as the woman who coyly extracted the secret to Samson's strength and betrayed him to the Philistines

Avoiding Selfish Pitfalls

Judges 16

Have you ever noticed that only a limited number of stories from Scripture seem to make it into all those colorful children's Bibles? There's the Creation, Noah and the Flood, David and Goliath, Jonah and the Whale, Jesus and the boy who loaned Him his lunch. These stories are usually adventures with several things in common—animals, fish, boats, giants, kids, and lunch.

Samson makes it into some of the collections, but not many. Why? He's the strongest man in the Bible, he played with animals, and he had lots of adventures. . . .

Maybe it's because Samson is actually a Bible story for grownups. Sure, he would look great in a cartoon movie—muscles bulging, hair flying, enemies running for their lives. But the real message of his life is hard to package into a bedtime story—sexual sin, betrayal, failed relationships, and a tragic, early death.

That brings us to Delilah, a woman whose name has come to mean "dangerous temptress." To a child, she may seem like an evil queen from a Disney plot, but adults see something else—and it's a lot scarier. In her we recognize much of what we fear in love relationships—deceptions, betrayals, and manipulations of every kind.

The story of Samson and Delilah happens during a dark time in Israel's history. It had been several hundred years since Joshua had invaded Canaan and divided up the spoils for the 12 tribes. The hard-won lessons from earlier days seem to have faded from the national memory. Israel was more a collection of quarreling clans than a nation. As a result, they were continually oppressed by stronger neighbors like the Philistines, a decadent and brutal people who lived along the Mediterranean coast.

During this time, Israel's leaders—called judges—were either priests or military heroes who helped administer laws and lead war parties. Samson, Israel's most famous judge, is one of only a handful of people in the Bible whose birth and life was predicted (others include Isaac, Jacob, John the Baptist, and Jesus).

Our story opens in Judges 13 with an angel's visit to a woman and her husband (Manoah). They would bear a son, he announced, who was to be "set apart to God from birth" (Judges13:2-24). Their son was to be raised according to strict religious and dietary rules and given into the Lord's service because he had a job to do—"he will begin the deliverance of Israel from the hands of the Philistines" (13:5).

Samson grew up with amazing physical strength. As a young warrior, he killed a lion with his bare hands, single-handedly burned and sacked Philistine towns, and wiped out a thousand enemy troops with only the jawbone of a donkey for a weapon (can you see the cartoon possibilities?). For the first time in generations, the Israelites began to feel like winners.

Samson led Israel for 20 years, and throughout his life, he delighted in taunting the enemy, who could never quite catch him.

Until Delilah.

For Samson, physical combat was an exciting risk, an adrenaline rush, a game—nothing more. And he always won. Unfortunately, he took the same attitude into his relationships with women. At stake in each "battle" was his calling as a servant of God.

But this was a truth Samson never grasped. As a result, his life came to its tragic climax, not on the battle front, but in the lap of a lover from the enemy camp.

Delilah used her powers of seduction and cajoling to find out the secret of Samson's great strength—his uncut hair. Then while Samson lay sleeping in her arms, she cut his hair and called in the Philistines to take him away. Samson tried to defend himself as before, but his strength had left him. The Philistines tied him up, gouged out his eyes, and threw him in prison.

The last scene from Samson's life takes place during a pagan celebration of his capture. Israel's judge and hero is humiliated—shackled and paraded for the pleasure of the crowd. Finally, standing between two pillars of Dagon's temple, Samson begins to pray. "O Sovereign Lord, remember me . . ." he cries out. "Please strengthen me just once more. . . ." Then he pushes against the pillars of the temple with all his might.

The temple cracks, then collapses in a roar, killing Samson along with thousands of his enemies.

What can married lovers today learn from this sensational and tragic couple? A lot. Even though Samson and Delilah were neither married nor successful in their relationship, their story brings a dramatic promise with it: If we're willing to learn from the fool in them, we can be rescued from the fool in us—before a trail of bad choices leads us into the lap of disaster.

He awoke from his sleep and thought, "I'll go out as before and shake myself free." But he did not know that the LORD had left him. Then the Philistines seized him, gouged out his eyes and took him down to Gaza.

—JUDGES 16:20-21

1 Blind Love

It's almost impossible to read the story of Samson and Delilah without mumbling, "Like they say, 'Love is blind!'" Surely only love could make a nation's leader sleep with the enemy, persuade a servant of God to betray lifelong vows, or trick a world-renowned muscle man into giving up his strength.

If ever there was a love that couldn't see the truth, it was Samson's.

But was it really love?

The Bible tells us that Samson "fell in love" with Delilah, but as any teenager learns, the word *love* covers a multitude of meanings. Yes, Samson was smitten. But the story clearly shows that his feelings were closer to infatuation or lust than love. And his consuming desire was no doubt fueled by deeper drives—pride, spiritual indifference, loneliness, maybe even a collision with mid-life.

It's true that an amazing blindness to the ordinary is the magic dust of a budding romance. But God's plan goes further. He hopes that what starts with self-centered desire will blossom into genuine love, a love that is blind—yes!—but blind to the shortcomings of the beloved.

In describing this kind of love, Paul could have written, *"Genuine love is blind to little annoyances (patient), blind to personal quirks (kind), blind to how good others may have it (does not envy),"* and so on.

Ultimately in our love relationship, we choose what to see and what to overlook. Samson's choices left him blind to Delilah's flattery and his own foolishness. He couldn't see that he had nothing to win but a little momentary pleasure—and he had everything to lose.

Today we can make another choice, knowing that genuine love is *not* love that *doesn't* see, but love that sees all—the flaws, shortcomings, selfishness, pride, and weaknesses of our partner—and yet loves. This kind of blindness doesn't happen by accident. But we can choose to cultivate it for our marriage every day.

> *Heavenly Father,*
>
> *Thank You that my spouse and I can enjoy the benefits of a relationship (including passionate attraction) inside the commitments of marriage. Today I ask You to help me see my partner's strengths and weaknesses through the eyes of love—Christ's love! Just as Paul prayed for the church, this is my prayer for my marriage today: "that your love may abound more and more in knowledge and depth of insight" (Philippians 1:9). Amen.*

 Identify one irritating behavior or weakness in your partner that you're willing to ask God to help you "go blind to" today for the sake of love.

Then Delilah said to Samson, "You have made a fool of me; you lied to me. Come now, tell me how you can be tied."

He said, "If anyone ties me securely with new ropes that have never been used, I'll become as weak as any other man."

—JUDGES 16:10-11

2 Juvenile Hang-Ups

Samson's string of dumb choices with Delilah wasn't the first time Samson had been duped into trusting a woman who betrayed his secrets—with almost equally disastrous results (read this story in Judges 14–16). How could a respected judge of Israel have such poor judgment in his personal life?

We've all met Samson before. He's that 40-year-old guy who's still running his life the same way he did when he was 17. We recognize Samson in the parade of talented celebrities who squander their promising futures with drugs or alcohol and end up in jail or dead.

And if we're honest, many of us recognize Samson's juvenile hang-ups in ourselves. We should have grown wiser by now, but we find ourselves still repeating the same mistakes over and over—a selfish habit, an easy manipulation, a private lust, a convenient irresponsibility.

Perhaps we can learn something from the choices that kept Samson behaving like a juvenile. For one thing, he loved excitement more than common sense. Those safe Jewish girls just couldn't make Samson's pulse race like Delilah did. Being in the wrong place at the wrong time became another way for him to get a thrill.

We often play with danger or tease ourselves with temptation for the same reasons. We feel more alive balancing on that high wire between pleasure and peril. But when we "stay to play" like Samson did we only get dumber, no matter how in-control we think we are. Wrong places and wrong impulses call for a simple strategy: *Run*. Remember Paul's advice to young Timothy—"Flee the evil desires of youth" (2 Timothy 2:22).

Another choice that hindered Samson's growth was that he didn't ask for or listen to anyone else's advice, not even his parents' (Judges 14:1-3). Delilah might have been a "tasty morsel," but Samson needed help to face the truth about what was really driving his reckless sexual hunger (was it selfishness, boredom, spiritual isolation?). We all need trusted friends who have our permission to be honest with us about the choices we're making.

No one knows our weaknesses better than our mate, and no relationship challenges immaturity more than marriage (no wonder it hurts so much at times). But so long as our helping efforts are wrapped in sincere love, we can motivate each other to leave juvenile ways behind. Our goal should be to imitate Epaphras, about whom Paul told the Colossians, "He is always wrestling in prayer for you that you may stand firm in all the will of God, mature and fully assured" (Colossians 4:12).

> *Heavenly Father,*
> *I really do need a life partner to say to me, "Let us stop going over the same old ground again and again. . . . Let us go on instead to other things and become mature in our understanding, as strong Christians ought to be"* (Hebrews 6:1, TLB). *Thank You for the opportunity to both give and receive this kind of encouragement today. Amen.*

Love Talk | Spend a few minutes today describing for your partner the mature aspects of his or her behavior you really appreciate. In what areas have you seen the most encouraging growth?

When Delilah saw that he had told her everything, she sent word to the rulers of the Philistines, "Come back once more. He has told me everything." So the rulers of the Philistines returned with the silver in their hands. Having put him to sleep on her lap, she called a man to shave off the seven braids of his hair, and so began to subdue him. And his strength left him.
—JUDGES 16:18-19

3 *Overexposed*

Of course Delilah knew before he said a word. She could see it in his eyes and hear it in his voice—*He's telling the truth now. He's finally coming out in the open.*

Those moments of personal exposure are often the ones we savor most in marriage. Somehow when the ordinary guy you're married to spills his guts about something that really matters, something that he's been protecting for years, he suddenly seems more endearing. Your wife's admission of an embarrassing insecurity makes you want to take her in your arms and hold her tight.

Marriage definitely puts us out in the breezy open with our mates. Our weaknesses and strengths, our oddities and ordinarinesses, our hopes and fears are all on display. Our partner has a lot to work with—and a choice. Such exposure invites understanding and intimacy—or it invites injury and regret.

Think about the choice Samson gave Delilah. In virtually the same breath he told her, "I can be a hero," and "I can be humiliated." Suddenly she was in a position to be Samson's trusted confidante—or a cruel traitor. If love had been in the picture, imagine the words that could have rushed to her lips: "Honey, thanks for talking. I understand you better now. I see who you are, and who you're meant to be. I'll help you—and I'll never tell your secret. . . ."

But instead Delilah reached for a razor and some rope. To her, winning, not Samson, was the prize.

Probably every day of our marriage we're given the opportunity to turn some intimate truth into an occasion for giving relief or encouragement to the one we love. Sometimes the greatest gift is to keep another's secrets locked away. In his book *The Mystery of Marriage,* Mike Mason says that love "creates safe ground." When a personal revelation happens in this kind of safety, breakthroughs—to sharing, understanding and trust—can begin.

Loyalty in what we do with what we know about another person is a foundation stone of all lasting relationships. No wonder Solomon wrote, "Let love and faithfulness never leave you" (Proverbs 3:3). "Love and faithfulness keep a king safe" (Proverbs 20:28).

Heavenly Father,

Today I want to receive and properly value what my beloved tells me—especially anything personally revealing or potentially damaging. My spouse is Your chosen child. Help me to use my tremendous power for his/her good. Amen.

Love Talk

Can you identify a particular circumstance where you are most likely to slip into being disloyal and hurtful with what you know about your spouse? What could you do to prepare for success instead of failure?

Then she said to him, "How can you say, 'I love you,' when you won't confide in me? This is the third time you have made a fool of me and haven't told me the secret of your great strength." With such nagging she prodded him day after day until he was tired to death.

—Judges 16:15-16

4 Power Moves

The drama of Judges 16 has often been portrayed as a lover's quarrel or a seduction scene. But it was really a duel of champions. Two powerful contestants held the fate of nations in their hands, both sides equally matched and ready.

In such confrontations, who is likely to win? Ask any martial arts teacher: the one who understands the enemy's weakness and can exploit it.

Delilah knew plenty about her man: This world-renowned muscle man would relish a physical contest. As an escape artist, he'd jump at a "tie-me-up" dare. And as an incorrigible playboy, he'd probably—like so many other men she'd met—leave his brains at the bedroom door.

What did Samson know about Delilah? Not much except that her loyalty was probably up for grabs. Yet he chose to focus on his desire for her (and the peace and quiet to enjoy her).

As the duel began, Delilah asked Samson to match his sexual intimacies with a personal revelation. When that didn't work, she let fly with a little shame ("you have made a fool of me"). Then she slapped a siege on his heart ("how can you say you love me when . . . ?"). And she never stopped pressing the attack ("with such nagging she prodded him day after day until he was tired to death").

For his part, Samson defended against Delilah's power moves like an overfed lion batting at a nap-time annoyance. . . .

Make the score for this battle of titans: Delilah—1; Samson—zip.

Let's step back from the story for a minute and think about our marriages. One of the most important questions we face is how to get what we want from our partner. Like the two in our story, we sometimes resort to power moves to make our spouse do or give us what we want:

- We use sex, comfort, gifts, or attention to get a desired response.

- We use words to win, regardless of how they might wound.

- We conveniently tell ourselves that if we don't lie by what we say, we're not lying by what we don't say.

- We carry around mixed loyalties (to other persons or priorities) that can get our marriages in a lot of trouble.

But maybe the really big gun of power moves is the *love* word itself. How many of us have said, "If you loved me you would . . ."? This might get you what you want at the moment, but rarely what you need.

Manipulation, whether it's nagging, pressuring, or deceit, is never an act of love. In marriage, if only one person wins, both lose.

Lord of Married Lovers,

Open my eyes today to things I do that might get me
what I want but will hurt my marriage in the long run.
Help me to lay down the weapons of selfishness and
pick up the building blocks of love. When I'm tempted
to manipulate or deceive, help me reach for honesty and
trust. When I try to change my partner, help me to
focus instead on what must change in me. Amen.

When do you feel manipulated by your spouse? Pick one issue that might be resolvable if you worked on it together ahead of time. For example, is there a way that you could meet his or her needs that would make a "power move" unnecessary?

So he told her everything. "No razor has ever been used on my head," he said, "because I have been a Nazirite set apart to God since birth."

—JUDGES 16:17

5 A Romantic Certainty

Samson was a Nazirite, set apart by God to begin the deliverance of Israel from the Philistines (Judges 13:5). But as he grew up and discovered his amazing gifts, something went wrong. He forgot that he wasn't the only person who mattered here. He forgot that his calling was ultimately intended by God for the benefit of others.

You might say Samson was embracing what psychologists call "the Romantic Fallacy." The term is usually used to explain how a baby views the universe. You see, when a baby is born, he thinks he *is* the universe. The baby can't distinguish where he ends and the world, including other people, begins. Eventually he figures out that Mom continues to exist when she is out of the room, and that she's a separate person. Still, she's very attentive. So the child settles on the view that though he does not *equal* the universe, he's definitely the center of it. As the child grows into adulthood, he eventually realizes that he is only one of many, equally significant people in the world.

However, some grownups are unable or unwilling to let go of the Romantic Fallacy—they still think everything revolves around them. And as a result, they make selfish and foolish choices without regard for how those decisions might affect others.

Samson's failure to consider his duty to his own people as he played a dangerous game on enemy territory is a good example of a man still clinging to the Romantic Fallacy.

All of us go through life wanting to be appreciated as one-of-a-kind creations with a unique place in the world. But if we look at the Bible carefully, we see God's answer to our longing. It's something we could call "the Romantic Certainty": *God loves the whole world equally, but He sent His Son Jesus for me personally.*

In God's eyes, each of us is a miracle from birth, blessed with special strengths, and set apart to fulfill a unique destiny during our lifetime. And in marriage, we're called to protect our beloved from self-centered thinking while blessing her or him with our full and devoted attention.

Together we can abandon any lingering romantic fallacies and embrace the romantic certainty God offers—that we, our spouse, and our marriage are all one-of-a-kind.

Incredible.

Not the center of the world, but anointed by God to make a difference in it.

> *Heavenly Father,*
> *Thank You that no matter how average my life and marriage looks today, your Spirit has chosen and anointed us for great things. Thank You that I'm loved by and special to You. What do You want to accomplish in me and my marriage today? How do You want to bless others through me? Show me, Lord. That is what I want with all my heart. Amen.*

Love Talk

Identify at least one gift in each of you that clearly sets you apart from others you know. Ask your spouse's opinion. How could this gift be a blessing to your marriage? How might it also represent a vulnerability?

CHAPTER SIX

Ruth & Boaz

About Ruth

Name: Means "friendship"
Age at Marriage: About 30
Appearance: Jewish tradition says she was beautiful
Personality: Loyal, hard-working, honest, sincere, brave
Family Background: A Moabitess from Moab, traditional enemy of Israel
Place in History: Famous for her loyalty to her mother-in-law and as the great-grandmother of David.

About Boaz

Name: Means "in him is strength"
Age at Marriage: About 50
Personality: Loyal, fair, generous, honorable optimistic
Family Background: Of the tribe of Judah, the clan of Elimelech, and in the lineage of Christ
Place in History: Obed (his son by Ruth) was the father of Jesse, and the grandfather of King David

Shaping a
Redemptive Marriage

The Book of Ruth

When you read the Bible, especially the Old Testament, it's hard to miss the fact that women usually got a raw deal. Generally, they are only mentioned if their kids or husbands were important (Hannah, the mother of Samuel; Sarah, the wife of Abraham), or if they were wicked in some particularly interesting way (Rahab, Delilah, Bathsheba, Gomer, and Mary Magdalene).

Most often, women were treated as family assets (e.g., "But Saul had given his daughter Michal, David's wife, to Paltiel . . ." (1 Samuel 25:44). Or as the spoils of war. Take, for example, the story of the Israelite civil war in Judges 19–21. The fight begins over the rape and butchery of a woman, and ends with more gender violence: "While the girls were dancing, each man caught one and carried her off to be his wife" (Judges 21:23).

Now turn the page in your Bible. Welcome to the book of Ruth . . .

After the brutality and moral decay that runs throughout Joshua and Judges, Ruth feels like a comforting evening at home by the fire. You might say the book of Ruth answers the question, "What would the Bible sound like if it were a story told by women and about women?"

Actually, the author of Ruth is unknown. But the tone and concerns of the story evoke a scene like this: Women have gathered around to talk while they work with their hands, sewing and mending. As they stitch pieces of fabric, they share news and gossip and opinions—about the new woman in town, the scarcity of good men, the problem with mother-in-laws, and that beautiful baby they held in the market just yesterday.

You can almost hear the women's voices in the opening lines of Ruth: "In the days when the judges ruled, there was a famine in the land, and a man from Bethlehem in Judah, together with his wife and two sons, went to live for a while in the country of Moab" (1:1).

The book begins by introducing us to Naomi, a woman who follows her husband to Moab, a neighboring country, only to watch him die. Her two grown sons take Moabite wives, but within ten years, the sons too are dead. The bereft Naomi decides it's time to go home to Bethlehem.

Daughter-in-law Ruth decides to go with her, even though as a foreigner from an enemy country, and a childless widow, Ruth's chances for remarriage in Israel are almost nil. Ruth's vow of loyalty is famous: "Where you go I will go, and where you stay I will stay. Your people will be my people and your God my God" (1:16).

With these words, Ruth becomes a full-fledged partner in Naomi's rather unpromising life. In many ways, Naomi is the forerunner of all sour-spirited mothers-in-law. When she arrives home, she announces that her new name should be "Mara," meaning "bitter." Five times in the first chapter Naomi blames God for her unhappiness:

- "the LORD's hand has gone out against me" (verse 13).

- "the Almighty has made my life very bitter" (verse 20).

- "the LORD has brought me back empty" (verse 21).

- "the LORD has afflicted me" (verse 21).

- "the Almighty has brought misfortune upon me" (verse 21).

In Bethlehem, the grain harvest is underway. Ruth goes to the field of an established farmer named Boaz to glean behind the workmen. It's the only food she and Naomi can find. But in the heat and dust of the fields, Ruth begins an acquaintance with Boaz, who as it turns out, is a relative of Naomi's on her deceased husband's side of the family.

When Naomi notices the extra attentions and kindnesses that Boaz lavishes on Ruth, hope returns, and a plan springs to her mind. It depends on two things:

- An ancient law whereby if a married man were to die without a son, one of his brothers was to marry the widow and bear children who would carry on the dead brother's name

- The honor and interest of Boaz

In one of Scripture's most memorable scenes, Ruth perfumes and prepares herself by lamplight under the watchful eye of Naomi, then goes to the community threshing floor where Boaz is spending the night. Boaz is asleep, and making sure no one sees her, Ruth lies down near him and waits.

Finally Boaz stirs, then sits up to notice a woman lying at his feet. "Who are you?" he asks, startled.

"I am your servant Ruth," she replies. "Spread the corner of your garment over me, since you are a kinsman-redeemer. . . ."

It's certainly the most moving marriage proposal in the Bible, and maybe in all of literature. And it is spoken by a woman. Hanging on Boaz's reply is hope and healing for both Ruth and Naomi.

Boaz doesn't keep her waiting. Not only is Boaz willing to become Ruth's kinsman-redeemer, he's delighted by her midnight proposal. He calls her request a kindness and a blessing, and vows to do everything in his power to make a wedding happen. . . .

It's hard for many of us today to imagine marrying our husband's brother. But the kinsman-redeemer practice was meant to provide for widows, guaranteeing them a future when they had none. And today it is a moving reminder of how God redeems each one of us with Christ's blood, and how He daily wants to turn our losses into gains.

If you read the story of Ruth closely, you see that Boaz began to "redeem" Ruth—making up for her lack—long before they were married.

- He gave her food (2:8-16).

- He protected her from other men (2:9).

- He affirmed her (2:11-12).

- He gave her dignity (2:15).

- He guarded her reputation (3:13-14).

- He "fought" for her (4:1-10).

The story reaches its happy conclusion with sounds all women love—of a wedding party, a baby's contented gurgling, and the excited conversations of visiting friends. Ruth's devotion to her mother-in-law has come full circle—now Naomi's care for Ruth has helped her meet and marry a loving husband. Now they can enjoy the pleasures of home and family and a secure future together.

No wonder this story of love in the fields holds such emotional power for husbands and wives today. In only four short chapters, we enter the lives of a man and two women who could easily be our neighbors, our relatives, maybe even ourselves. Like us, they find companionship, love, and healing through the gift of marriage. Their stories of redemption remind us that it is God's nature to always be at work in our lives. He is the one who can turn sorrows, losses—even death—into hope.

Don't urge me to leave you or to turn back from you. Where you go I will go, and where you stay I will stay. Your people will be my people and your God my God. Where you die I will die, and there I will be buried. May the LORD deal with me, be it ever so severely, if anything but death separates you and me.
—*Ruth* (RUTH 1:15-17)

"I Will Go with You"

Imagine you have traveled back in time. From a great distance, looking out across the sweep of the treeless plateau, you notice a dirt road cutting the scene east to west, and on the road, three black dots. The dots are people, you can tell, moving west. They are dressed in black, and yes, it's clear they are women. As unlikely as it seems, you decide you're watching a migration of widows.

Take your imaginary viewpoint closer: Now you're beside the road, up to your chin in ripening wheat. Insects whir and sing. The widows approach, stopping and starting. Their conversation seems agitated. Another stop. One throws her arms around the other, wails, then returns the way she has come.

The remaining two keep talking and gesturing as they come closer. You see that the face of one is craggy, sunburned. The face of the other is flushed but smooth, too young by far to be wearing widows' black.

When you can finally hear what the younger one is saying, your jaw drops. They're exchanging . . . *wedding vows?!*

Kind of a shock to modern readers! But Ruth's speech on that road to nowhere has become one of the best-known declarations of married love in the Christian world. It's a wedding favorite, even though it was delivered by one widow to another, each of whom had put away hopes for marriage.

Let's look at the outline of Ruth's commitment to her mother-in-law. We could call it "The Vows of a Shared Life":

- *"I will share your journey."* Ruth promises the gift of her presence—"wherever you go, I will go" (no qualifiers like ". . . unless you decide to teach junior high or live in Cleveland").

- *"I will share your family."* Ruth promises to accept Naomi's family and heritage as her own (no, "But I refuse to deal with Aunt Betty").

- *"I will share your values and your spiritual commitment."* Ruth promises to set aside whatever she had valued or worshiped and adopt her mother-in-law's God (no, "You believe what you want, and so will I").

- *"I will share your life always."* Ruth promises to stay with Naomi, no matter what, until death (no, "I'll stay committed to you as long as I'm growing personally").

In *Finding the Love of Your Life,* counselor Neil Clark Warren says every strong marriage is built on unconditional promises. "On the basis of commitment, you can soar together on the wings of unnegotiated love. *This* is the kind of love that can provide 'lift' to your relationship. You are not held together by relational successes but by a 'blood covenant.' And that kind of covenant makes for deep inner security."

Some distance back on the road you're traveling, you and your spouse made promises to share your lives until death. Friends and family and God Himself were watching. Those vows can still be wings to help you soar today.

Lord,

Thank You for the remarkable loyalty of Ruth. And thank You for the life partner You have brought me. May I keep my vows of a shared life today with all my heart—for Your honor, and my good, and the blessing of my marriage. Amen.

 Elizabeth Barrett Browning wrote, "If I leave all for thee, wilt thou exchange and be all for me?" How is the "exchange" working in your marriage today?

And Ruth the Moabitess said to Naomi, "Let me go to the fields and pick up the leftover grain behind anyone in whose eyes I find favor." . . . *As it turned out, she found herself working in a field belonging to Boaz.*

—RUTH 2:2-3

2 Second Chances

When Ruth decided to follow Naomi to Bethlehem, she pretty much botched her chances of finding a new husband. In fact, if Ruth had taken out a personal ad in her new home, it might have read something like this:

> **Foreign Attraction.** Single widow with Green Card looking for husband in good health. Kids probably not an option. I'm a hard worker with limited resources. Sorry, but unhappy mother-in-law comes with.

It's easy to see why Naomi urged her to do the "smart" thing: "Go home to your own family. I can't help you." Instead, Ruth chose to follow her heart, her conscience, and her new-found God. As a result, she got what she so desperately needed—a second chance at love, family, and home.

Some of us who are remarried understand how precious a second chance at love can be. Others of us desperately need a second chance within the marriage we have—another try at intimacy, faithfulness, and righting wrongs. How can we get back on the road to grace, restoration, and renewal?

Although at first glance it appears Ruth just got lucky, a closer look reveals that she put herself directly in the path of God's blessing. It was because she was humble enough to beg that she came to work in the field of her husband-to-be. And it was through her willingness to risk her own happiness that she won Boaz's admiration before he ever laid eyes on her.

Recall his words to her: "I've been told all about what you have done for your mother-in-law since the death of your husband—how you left your father and mother and your homeland and came to live with a people you did not know before. May the LORD repay you for what you have done. May you be richly rewarded by the LORD, the God of Israel, under whose wings you have come to take refuge" (Ruth 2:11-12).

In what areas of your marriage do you and your partner both need a second chance with each other and with God today? Where has trust been lost, loyalties compromised, or laziness taken the place of passion? Where do you need God to restore what years of neglect have destroyed?

How good to know that God is in the business of second chances. As He so clearly demonstrated by His patience with Israel's many rebellions, His mercy extends far beyond our failures. Paul put it this way, "Where sin increased, grace increased all the more" (Romans 5:20).

The prophet Joel looked past Israel's present troubles and foretold of a restoration to come. His prophecy echoes Ruth's renewal experience: "The threshing floors will be filled with grain; the vats will overflow with new wine and oil. I will repay you for the years the locusts have eaten. . . . You will have plenty to eat until you are full, and you will praise the name of the LORD your God, who has worked wonders for you . . ." (Joel 2:24-26).

Today, if we're willing to seek God with all our hearts, we too can be confident that He will work wonders of restoration for us and our marriage.

> *God of Second Chances,*
>
> *How grateful I am that You do not give up on me even when I lose sight of the good You want to accomplish in our marriage. Show me where I need restoration in my relationship with my spouse. Help me to ask humbly for another chance in areas where I've failed, perhaps repeatedly. And give me Ruth's heart of courage and faith. Amen.*

 Have you experienced what felt like a second chance from your mate and/or from God? How did you cooperate to help that happen?

Ruth approached quietly, uncovered his feet and lay down. In the middle of the night something startled the man, and he turned and discovered a woman lying at his feet.

"Who are you?" he asked.

"I am your servant Ruth," she said. "Spread the corner of your garment over me, since you are a kinsman-redeemer."

—RUTH 3:7-9

3 *"I Need You"*

Ruth's midnight proposal to Boaz on the threshing floor stands in stark contrast with other marriage stories in the Bible. She did the asking. She had no father or brother to negotiate a bride-price and no lavish gifts of jewelry were exchanged.

And while brides such as Rachel and Rebekah had plenty to offer—youth, beauty, the right family, financial security, and potential for producing heirs—Ruth didn't. She was widowed, a foreigner, assumed to be barren, and almost destitute.

The setting for Ruth's proposal wasn't exactly romantic either. A threshing floor, probably a communal one. The word *love* is never even mentioned. Perhaps that is because it wasn't necessary. Love, in this case, was not about romance or passion. It was about a deeply felt need met with a compassionate response, which added up to redemption.

Like Ruth, all of us bring some form of poverty to our marriage—a broken past, an aching hunger, or deep personality flaws. Some days we may feel we have nothing to bring to love's exchange but need. We crouch at our mate's feet and wonder: *When my mate discovers who I really am, will I be claimed or rejected?*

117

But this is the redemptive moment God waits for—when one lover is brave enough to say, *"I need you, and it will cost you something,"* and the other is willing to say, *I see who you are—and what commitment will cost—and I still want you!"*

Charles Morgan once wrote, "There is no surprise more magical than the surprise of being loved; it is God's finger on man's shoulder."

Love that comes to you when you feel worthy of it is a wonderful thing. But love you don't expect, love that covers over a lack or an injury, love that replaces what's missing—that experience of love is priceless. It heals us.

How can we practice this kind of redemptive love in marriage? Synonyms for *redeem* include: to restore, to recover, to reclaim. Quietly consider your spouse's areas of need for a moment. How can you help to restore something he or she is lacking? Maybe it's confidence in their parenting, or an assurance of their attractiveness. How can you help your spouse recover from an old wound or a troubling habit? What has been lost that you can help reclaim—a dream, a hobby, a relationship with a family member?

Then ask God to help you find a way to tap the one you love on the shoulder today.

> *My Lord and My Redeemer,*
> *You have answered my prayers to cover me with Your mercy and grace and acceptance. Let me be the one who says yes to that plea for covering today. Help me be part of the restoring, recovering and reclaiming that are Your plan for the one I love. Amen.*

 Tell each other one sensitive area where you need covering today.

Then Ruth told her mother-in-law about the one at whose place she had been working. "The name of the man I worked with today is Boaz," she said.

"The LORD bless him!" Naomi said to her daughter-in-law. "He has not stopped showing his kindness to the living and the dead." She added, "That man is our close relative; he is one of our kinsman-redeemers."

—RUTH 2:19-20

4 A Gentleman Farmer

Boaz's appearance on the scene reawakens hope in Naomi's heart and is the crucial turning point of this story. Suddenly, Naomi realizes that though her dead sons have no brothers, there may yet be a kinsman who can redeem Ruth. She hopes to provide for her own future this way, too.

The kinsman-redeemer practice (also called a levirate marriage) is described in Deuteronomy 25:5-6. If a married man died without a son, the law prescribed that one of his brothers was to marry the widow and bear children by her to carry on the dead brother's name. The kinsman was to "redeem"—buy back—any of the deceased man's property as well, which the firstborn son would then inherit. Originally the levirate marriage only applied to brothers. But by Ruth's time, it had extended to include any "next of kin."

As Ruth's kinsman-redeemer, Boaz was fulfilling a legal duty when he married her. But Boaz went much further than the law required.

Boaz held all the cards. Yet, when he approached Ruth as she was gleaning in his fields, he protected her dignity, complimented her on her reputation, and let her know how honored he felt to have her work in his fields. Then, rather than embarrass her with charity, he instructs his reapers to drop extra grain for her to gather.

Later, when Ruth is at her most vulnerable—crouching at his feet and "proposing" a levirate marriage—Boaz again acts as if it is she who is doing him the favor: "The LORD bless you, my daughter," he replied. "This kindness is greater than that which you showed earlier: You have not run after the younger men, whether rich or poor" (Ruth 3:10).

In many ways, Boaz is the Old Testament's consummate gentleman (what a contrast in such barbaric times!). His tender approach is a great example for couples today. Our marriages are full of duties and obligations to one another: Who will be responsible for getting the taxes done? Who will clean and cook? Who will shuttle kids to practice?

Boaz reminds us to ask: With what love, consideration, and tenderness do I fulfill my duties? And when I give to my spouse, do I make it an affirmation, not an embarrassment, to be on the receiving end? This gentleman farmer turned duty into love, and consideration into redemption.

Through Boaz, God gives us a picture of Himself as a loving redeemer. Isaiah described how God's care for us rescues us from past losses and sorrows: "You will forget the shame of your youth and remember no more the reproach of your widowhood. For your Maker is your husband—the Lord Almighty is his name— the Holy One of Israel is your Redeemer . . ." (Isaiah 54:4-5).

Lord,

Let me learn from the example of Boaz—to think of the needs of my spouse, to give graciously, to believe in Your future for both of us, even when it's hard to see. Thank You for Your love, O Redeeming God. Amen.

Someone has written: "Duty says, 'You must.' Love says, 'I must.' Duty creeps; love has wings." Turn one duty into an affirming gift of love today—then talk this evening about how it made each of you feel.

The women said to Naomi: "Praise be to the LORD, who this day has not left you without a kinsman-redeemer. May he become famous throughout Israel! He will renew your life and sustain you in your old age. For your daughter-in-law, who loves you and who is better to you than seven sons, has given him birth.

—RUTH 4:14-15

5 *Generation to Generation*

This is the second of two powerful tributes in this story concerning Ruth's devotion to her mother-in-law (the first being Boaz's praise upon meeting Ruth). Naomi must have been delighted to hear Ruth referred to as "better than seven sons"—an astounding statement, because having seven sons (symbolizing the number of completeness) was considered the epitome of family blessing in Israel.

So how did Ruth earn such high praise?

She provided for her mother-in-law. Ruth went out to beg for grain to feed them both (Ruth 2:2-3). In sharp contrast, we often spend more time worrying about our next vacation than about helping our parents. But the Bible's dictate hasn't changed: "If a widow has children or grandchildren, these should learn first of all to put their religion into practice by caring for their own family and so repaying their parents and grandparents" (1 Timothy 5:4).

She respected Naomi's advice. She listened when Naomi advised her to stay in Boaz's fields (Ruth 2:22-23), and again, when Naomi told her how to approach Boaz on the threshing floor. God's Word makes it clear that wisdom comes with age (Job 12:12), and the Fifth Commandment tells us to honor our parents (Exodus 20:12). What better way to honor them than to ask, "What do you think?"

She confided in Naomi. Ruth talked with Naomi about her day, Boaz's treatment, and then told her "everything" that happened when she "proposed." How much our own parents and in-laws, even if they don't live nearby, love to feel included and informed. Do we take time to include them in our life, to tell them everything?

She loved her mother-in-law. Because Naomi's friends refer to Ruth as "your daughter-in-law who loves you" (Ruth 4:15), we know that Ruth wasn't resentful or just going through the motions of caring for her mother-in-law. She *genuinely* loved her and must have expressed this in visible ways.

She gave Naomi a substantial role in caring for baby Obed. The Bible is full of happy in-laws, but none so happy as Naomi who "took the child, laid him in her lap and cared for him." In fact, her friends went so far as to say, "Naomi has a son." How generous are we with our parents and extended family when it comes to sharing our children?

Ruth and Boaz's love story illustrates how our marriages—and our children—are not meant only for our own happiness, but also for that of our family. Though our relationships with parents and in-laws can sometimes be challenging, God will bless the couple who honors their family, even when it seems difficult to do so.

> Lord,
> Both of us want to live out our faith by being a blessing to our extended families, especially our in-laws. Teach us the loyalty of Ruth so that we too might care deeply and sacrificially for the parents who gave us life. May we honor and provide for them as long as they live. Amen.

Love Talk | What can each of you do today to love the other's parents?

CHAPTER SEVEN

Hannah & Elkanah

About Hannah

Name: Means "gracious"
Age at Marriage: Probably late twenties, early thirties
Appearance: Unknown
Personality: Passionate, intense, devout,
   true to her word
Family Background: Parents unknown,
   wife of Elkanah
Place in History: Mother of the prophet Samuel

About Elkanah

Name: Means "God has possessed"
Age at Marriage: Unknown, probably late thirties
Appearance: Unknown
Personality: Patient, gentle, kind, devout
Family Background: From the tribe of Levi
Place in History: Father of the prophet Samuel

Nurturing Spiritual Unity

1 Samuel 1–2

To watch the story of Hannah and Elkanah unfold, you would hardly need to go to their home in Ramah. Most of the action takes place in the temple courtyard at Shiloh, a worship center located in the hills north of Jerusalem. (Remember, this was in the days before Solomon built the temple in Jerusalem.) But even though this couple's experience turns on deeply spiritual questions, we see everything from a completely human viewpoint—a husband's gesture at mealtime, a wife's tears, another woman's snide remark, a toddler's new coat.

If you were progressing through the Bible front to back, you might recognize something familiar about the tone of Hannah and Elkanah's story. That's because it is told with the same quiet restraint as the love story that just precedes it in the Bible, the story of Ruth and Boaz. In both accounts, a humble yet determined woman, with the help of an honorable and sensitive husband, overcomes great obstacles to bear a child—who then turns out to be someone famous in Israel's history (Ruth becomes the great-grandmother of David; Hannah, the mother of Samuel). And both stories occur at nearly the same turning point in Israel's history, when Israel is about to change from rule by judges to rule by kings. At this critical moment in time, God focuses not on the famous or powerful, but on two marriages, and the children that result.

When the story opens, we meet Elkanah, a pious man with two wives. Every year at harvest time, he takes his wives and children to worship at the religious festival at Shiloh. But every year the trip becomes more painful. While one wife, Peninnah, keeps having more children, the other wife, Hannah, remains barren. Every year at baby dedication time, her arms seem emptier. To make matters worse, Peninnah mocks Hannah for her infertility.

When Elkanah finds his wife crying one night, he tries rather clumsily to comfort her. "Aren't I more important to you than ten sons?" he asks.

Years pass, but the scene at Shiloh hasn't changed. Finally Hannah reaches bottom. Standing near a sacrificial altar, she starts to pray aloud—and to make a most severe pledge: "Lord, if you would only notice my misery and answer my pleas for a son, then I would give him back to you as your servant for his whole life!"

Will God answer? If he does, will Hannah keep her vow? How will her husband react? And what is the significance in the long run?

The answer to these questions introduces the theme of spiritual unity in marriage, which plays an important part of this story. For example, during the course of this brief, two-chapter story, the couple:

- Demonstrate the importance of regular worship attendance.

- Support each other's spiritual commitments, even when it hurts.

- Put a high priority on thankfulness and praise to God.

- Demonstrate the power of prayer and obedience.

- Illustrate unity in their parenting decisions.

Indeed, God does answer Hannah's prayer and she conceives a son. And as she and Elkanah make good on her vow concerning Baby Samuel, we are given a rare portrait of a deeply spiritual couple. Through faith and their devotion to each other, Hannah and Elkanah were strong enough to give back to God what they surely most wanted to keep.

*Year after year this man [Elkanah] went up
from his town to worship and sacrifice to the
LORD Almighty at Shiloh.*

—1 SAMUEL 1:3

1 Together at Shiloh

If you were going to make a list of Bible heroes, Elkanah probably wouldn't even get nominated. He could never compete with celebrity names like Moses, David, or Paul. But that would probably suit this quiet man just fine.

You see, Elkanah was a low-profile plodder—no big ambitions, reputation, or connections in sight. He was just a regular guy.

But you could count on him. If something was important, Elkanah didn't quit on it. And caring for the spiritual life of his marriage and family was important to Elkanah.

He took his family to worship and sacrifice at Shiloh regularly. He wasn't just following the crowd either. Remember, this was during a time of corruption and spiritual deadness in Israel's history, where "everyone did as he saw fit" (Judges 17:6).

As their love story unfolds, we see how the spiritual unity Elkanah and Hannah enjoyed made a huge difference in their marriage. They stood together in worship, in petition, in waiting, and in tears. When Hannah made a radical promise to give her baby back to God, Elkanah stood by her again. Why? Their love was anchored in eternity, not circumstances (2 Corinthians 4:18).

They really *believed* that the Lord would "make good his word" (1 Samuel 1:23).

A flourishing spiritual life is often the hardest part of a marriage to nurture, especially when trials come. But from the quiet example of Elkanah and Hannah we can learn the importance of:

- Making regular worship a family priority.

- Pursuing our own relationship with God.

- Supporting each other's spiritual journey.

- Trusting together in God's goodness—no matter what the circumstances or the cost.

Maybe we should rethink our "Bible heroes" list. Elkanah simply set out to be a godly man his wife could count on "year after year." But God used him to make history (and a beautiful marriage). If that isn't heroic, what is?

> Lord,
>   Forgive me for letting so many daily "priorities" keep me from nurturing our spiritual life together. Without your Spirit at work in our marriage, we can't build anything that will last. Show us what we can do today to treasure and obey the Spirit in our home. Amen.

 Can you think of one expression or action that would build spiritual unity in your marriage today?

Whenever Hannah went up to the house of the LORD, her rival provoked her till she wept and would not eat. Elkanah her husband would say to her, "Hannah, why are you weeping? Why don't you eat? Why are you downhearted? Don't I mean more to you than ten sons?"

—1 SAMUEL 1:7-8

2 A Comfort that Comforts

One of the most touching scenes in Hannah's story is when Elkanah tries to comfort her. He was obviously in earnest. The Bible doesn't tell us to what extent he was successful, but we can learn something from studying his approach.

What did Elkanah do right? First, he noticed his wife's unhappiness. This means that Elkanah was paying attention to Hannah and was sensitive to her moods. And when he noticed her unhappiness, he responded by expressing concern for her. Most important of all, Elkanah let Hannah know that he valued their love relationship despite all the disappointments life had brought to their marriage.

We can also learn from the mistakes Elkanah may have made. Some people read Elkanah's comments, "Why are you weeping? Why don't you eat?" as a failure to identify with her feelings of sadness.

How many of us have ever said to our mate, "Hey, it's not that bad. Look at what you still have."

In a similar way, Elkanah's statement, "Don't I mean more to you than ten sons?"—while affirming his desire for relationship with Hannah—could also be interpreted as, "Hey, if you really loved me I'd be enough to make you happy! Come on and perk up!" Another easy, but unhelpful approach.

So what can we do to best comfort a troubled spouse?

Paul wrote to the Galatians, "Carry each other's burdens . . ." (Galatians 6:2). To comfort our mates, we must also *share*—enter into—their griefs. When our mate is depressed, sad, or confused, we help best when we:

- Listen. Ask your mate how he or she feels, and then repeat back what you've heard in order to show that you really heard.

- Affirm. Agree with your spouse that there is good cause to be sad. Show you understand he or she is not making too much of a small thing.

- Allow. Each person takes a different amount of time to process pain. Be patient with the extent and duration of your spouse's sorrows.

The art of comforting takes time and patience. But to be met in our grief by one who cares, by the one closest to us, is to feel the compassion and healing touch of Christ.

> *Lord and Comforter,*
> *Help us today to be compassionate with one another,*
> *to bear each other's burdens, and to share our sorrows*
> *with each other and with You. We can comfort each*
> *other, but You alone bring the healing that we need.*
> *Help us to draw comfort from You, so that we can com-*
> *fort each other with Your love. Amen.*

 Love Talk | Discuss how differently each of you grieve or show sadness. Do you cry? Do you withdraw? How can your partner best comfort and help?

"After the boy is weaned, I will take him and present him before the LORD, and he will live there always."

"Do what seems best to you," Elkanah her husband told her. ". . . Only may the LORD make good his word."

—1 SAMUEL 1:22-23

3 "You Did What?"

Imagine for a moment that you and your wife have been unable to conceive a child. Then one day your wife comes home from church and says, "Honey, today I pleaded with God for a baby, and I promised Him that if He granted me one I would give the child to a missionary pastor and his wife to be raised in the service of the Lord."

Most of us would blurt out something like, "You did *what?* That's my baby too, you know."

Although most of us will never deal with our mate giving away one of our children to God, we've all faced this issue on a smaller scale. Hank comes home with a grin on his face and announces to his wife, "I just bought a boat!" Or Shelley announces to Bill over dinner that she invited her parents to join them on vacation ("Oh honey—really, it'll be fine!" she says, before he's even managed to inhale).

Even if our mate's choices turn out OK, we still feel that something basic—a foundational agreement of our marriage—has been violated: *We're together in this. Any major decision that affects us both, requires us both.* We would expect a conversation beforehand, and we would strive for agreement.

132

It's only fair to ask why Hannah felt the freedom to act alone in such a crucial matter. And, when, if ever, is such a risk reasonable in marriage? In Hannah and Elkanah's story we find some sensible guidelines:

1. We should make sure we are acting on our mate's trust, not violating it. Hannah obviously knew that Elkanah would understand her vow and had great faith in her spiritual judgment. This is evidenced by Elkanah's answer when she explains her plans to leave Samuel at the temple—"Do what seems best to you," he says.

2. We should test our motives. Hannah wasn't being manipulative, defiant, or purposely trying to leave out Elkanah. Her decision wasn't motivated by selfish gain, but by a sincere spiritual encounter with God. Hannah may well have reasoned that her loyalty was first of all to God, then to her husband.

3. We should act on the basis of shared values. Hannah knew of Elkanah's devotion to the Lord—he had proved it every year of their married life (1 Samuel 1:3-5). Also, most commentators believe that Elkanah was from the tribe of Levi. For him, then, temple service would have had a long and honored tradition among his relatives. Hannah understood that dedicating their son to the Lord's service would seem an honor, not a loss, for her husband.

Consider some other important arenas of marriage:

- Finances
- Social activities and relationships
- Relatives
- Raising children
- Use of time, especially free time or family time

Do you and your spouse have an understanding about decision-making in each of these areas? For example, do you need to consult each other before one of you invites friends to dinner? Before you make an unexpected purchase over $50?

Because not every decision we make in marriage falls into a neat category, there is much to be said for nurturing trust and confidence in each other's motivations and judgments. In 1 Corinthians 4:2, God reminds us that "it is required that those who have been given a trust must prove faithful."

And what a powerful bond a man and woman form when such confidence is present! Each is freed and empowered, as Hannah was, to face critical personal decisions boldly.

How boldly? Hannah could give back to God the very gift she had waited so long for, confident that her Lord was good—and that her husband was standing right by her side.

> *Heavenly Father,*
> *Strengthen my dear mate and me today—not so that we can succeed separately, but that we can become strong together. We need to learn to be united in our decisions. Help us to put down anything that gets in the way of the oneness You have in mind: pride, stubbornness, the desire to be right, selfishness, an exaggerated sense of self-importance. Amen.*

 Can you trace any recent disagreements in your marriage back to a breakdown in decision-making? Was it a misunderstanding or an outright violation? Take a little time to help the other understand your needs and expectations.

I prayed for this child, and the LORD has granted me what I asked of him. So now I give him to the LORD. For his whole life he will be given over to the LORD."

—1 SAMUEL 1:27-28

4 With Open Hands

This is a scene to make any mother's heart quiver. Hannah is standing in front of the old priest Eli, holding the hand of a three-year-old boy, her only child. "I am the woman who . . . ," she begins.

Eli peers at her, probably trying unsuccessfully to remember her name, her story.

The child fidgets. He stares up at the priest's bushy white eyebrows, hugs his mother's leg, thinks about home—anything so he doesn't have to look over at the altar where a lamb lies bleeding.

His name is Samuel. He is a miracle—the answer to his mother's desperate plea on these very courtyard stones. And now, as part of her astonishing vow, the little boy is about to be left here while Mom goes home alone, keeping her vow at the cost of her son. . . .

Talk about making parents uncomfortable! *Just leave this child? After all those years of prayers and longing? Why, even God couldn't possibly want that to happen.*

Hannah's example of radical devotion to God and utter trust in His goodness has moved generations of parents. Maybe one reason is that we understand so well the agony of split loyalties: mother to child, wife to husband, woman to God.

135

But behind the dramatic conflict of Hannah's story, Christian parents sense an even more fundamental truth. *Our children belong to God from birth.* Not in theory, but in fact.

With that statement comes a feeling of . . . well . . . loss. Look at it this way: We fall in love and marry to add to our lives—affection, companionship, sexual fulfillment, security. Thereafter, most of us want children to add to our marriages.

But Hannah's story reminds us that all God's gifts are on loan—ourselves, our marriages, and our kids. And, contrary to our human way of thinking, fulfillment doesn't come from stubbornly clutching God's gifts to our chests. To follow God, we must hold our treasures loosely, in open hands—ready to let God use them for His glory.

Such a big part of parenting together in a marriage is giving our children back to God every day. God seemed to know that this demanding aspect of parenting would work best with two partners standing side by side.

> *Heavenly Father,*
> *You know what it's like to have a son, to watch Him grow up in the world, and to let Him go. Help my spouse and I to surround our children with love, even in imperfect circumstances, confident that You are their Father too. And every day, may our children grow in maturity and favor with You and others. Amen.*

Love Talk

Peter Ustinov once said, "We are the bones on which our children sharpen their teeth." Can you and your spouse identify a current parenting experience that, though painful, might be a natural part of the "growing up and letting go" process? How can you encourage each other through this challenge?

Whenever the day came for Elkanah to sacrifice, he would give portions of the meat to his wife Peninnah and to all her sons and daughters. But to Hannah he gave a double portion because he loved her, and the LORD had closed her womb.

—1 SAMUEL 1:4-5

5 Small Things

Scripture tells us nothing about the courtship of Elkanah and Hannah. We don't know anything about what they looked like, their engagement, or the occasion of the wedding.

Clearly, when God took time to share this love story, He wasn't so much interested in the sparks and swooning aspects of love, as in the kind of mature married love that can outlast life's troubles.

What Scripture does provide is a record of little deeds and great faith. Elkanah's devotion shines through in his sensitivity to Hannah's grief over her childlessness. He could have shamed her for "inadequacies," or even divorced her. Instead he loved Hannah for *who* she was far more than for *what* she could or could not give him.

And so Elkanah tried to fill her emptiness with gifts of comfort, affirmation, and honor. The extra portion he gave to her "because he loved her," might sound trivial. But it was a tender act, worthy of being recorded in the Bible for all time.

Suppose that Paul had Elkanah in mind when he wrote to the Ephesians, "Be completely humble and gentle; be patient, bearing with one another in love" (Ephesians 4:2). The apostle, as he wrote, might have been imagining Elkanah stooping down to love his wife. With what—a new house? A miracle cure? A new wardrobe? No, it was only an extra ladle of stew. But the ladle said, "You're so special to me," or maybe, "God keeps His promises— you'd better start eating for two!"

To Hannah at that moment, her husband's stew must have tasted something like God's nearness and love.

Look at the key words of Paul's advice again: *humble, gentle, patient.* There is so much good encouragement for marriage in the words of that one sentence that we could call Ephesians 4:2 the recipe for a happy marriage.

What will you choose to include in your marriage recipe today? What one token of love—a gesture, a private remark, a surprising affirmation, an overdue apology—could you give to the one you love?

Today God invites us to remember that Elkanah was right: Small tokens of love given with great faithfulness make way for God's miracles.

> *Dear Father,*
> *So many things are beyond my control to change or improve. But help me to see what is within my power— those little words, choices, and actions that would make all the difference in my marriage. Lord, Elkanah's humble service to his wife and his quiet faith in their future were beautiful gifts to his marriage. Show me how I can give those same gifts today. And help me to do it. Amen.*

 In your search for a love token to give your spouse, focus on what's near-at-hand—something he or she has perhaps said or asked for before. Ask God to help you see the obvious.

CHAPTER EIGHT

David & His Wives

About David

Name: Means "beloved"

Appearance: Ruddy, handsome, athletic

Personality: Emotional, reflective, brave, devoted to God, a leader

Family Background: Grew up near Bethlehem, herded sheep as a boy

Place in History: The boy who killed Goliath; the "man after God's own heart;" author of many psalms; Israel's greatest king

About Michal

Name: Means "who is like God?"

Age at Marriage: Probably about 15

Appearance: Probably tall; dark and striking like her father, Saul

Personality: Prideful, concerned with appearances, but devoted to David

Family Background: Grew up in Israel's first royal family

Place in History: The wife who was jealous of her husband's devotion to God

About Abigail

Name: Means "cause of joy"

Age at Marriage: Perhaps early twenties

Appearance and Personality: Intelligent, beautiful, poised, wise

Family Background: Unknown; widow of Nabal, a well-to-do farmer

Place in History: The woman who convinced David not to take vengeance on her wicked husband Nabal

About Bathsheba

Name: Means "daughter of an oath"

Age at Marriage: About 20

Appearance: Said to be "very beautiful"

Personality: Regal, strong, determined

Family Background: A daughter of one of David's bodyguards; wife of Uriah, one of his warriors

Place in History: The woman with whom King David committed adultery after he glimpsed her bathing on her roof

Guarding Your Heart

1 Samuel 18, 25
2 Samuel 3–6, 22, 25
1 Kings 1

"Renaissance man," *noun*—a person who is highly skilled in a wide range of the arts and sciences. In the Old Testament, no one would fit that description better than David. Just look at his résumé:

- Giant slayer (1 Samuel 17)
- Harpist (1 Samuel 16:18)
- Bear and lion fighter (1 Samuel 17:36)
- Songwriter/poet (2 Samuel 22 and many psalms)
- Desert commando and cave dweller (1 Samuel 22:12)
- King (2 Samuel 5:1-12)
- Skilled shepherd (1 Samuel 17:34-35)
- Spiritual leader (1 Chronicles 16, 28)
- Amateur astronomer (Psalm 8, 19:1-6)
- General (1 Chronicles 18-20)
- Politician (2 Samuel 19-21)
- Man of prayer (1 Chronicles 17:16-27 and many psalms)
- Architect (1 Chronicles 22:7)

Add to this impressive list of credentials that he was a gorgeous specimen of manhood (1 Samuel 16:12), and it is no wonder artists of the Italian Renaissance so frequently painted and sculpted this Jewish hero as the ideal man. In 1501, when Michelangelo got hold of the most coveted chunk of pure white marble Florence had seen in years (18 feet high and weighing several tons), he set about to carve one man—David, with "all the most heroic qualities in all young heroes."

Between Moses and Christ, no one else strides across the pages of the Old Testament history with such a commanding presence. In reality, David was far from an ideal man. He committed adultery, arranged for an innocent man's murder, and was a failure as a father. One of his blunders cost Israel 70,000 lives. Yet he could pray,

> Search me, O God, and know my heart;
> test me and know my anxious thoughts.
> See if there is any offensive way in me,
> and lead me in the way everlasting (Psalm 139:23-24).

Just browse through the book of Psalms—much of which reads like David's spiritual journal— and you know that David was a passionate man. He pursued his life and his devotion to God with intensity and sometimes with reckless abandon.

No surprise then that this man of deep emotion could easily win the title of the Bible's greatest lover. In fact, David married at least eight wives.

Fortunately, the three women whom we meet in the Bible accounts—Michal, Abigail, and Bathsheba—are fascinating personalities themselves. If we can get past the cultural unfamiliarity of having multiple wives in one marriage, we'll be rewarded with many helpful insights.

Michal, Princess—Wife of David's Youth
(1 Samuel 18; 2 Samuel 3–6)

David's marriage to Michal, his first, is probably best remembered for the 100 Philistine foreskins Saul demanded as a brideprice (hoping to see David killed in meeting his end of the bargain). But despite a glamorous start—national hero weds king's daughter—their marriage seemed doomed almost from the start. Their romance begins with the words: "Now Saul's daughter Michal was in love with David, and when they told Saul about it, he was pleased. 'I will give her to him,' he thought, 'so that she may be a snare to him . . .'" (1 Samuel 18:20-21).

But the marriage of the young couple was up against more than just a hateful father. Their relationship suffered through years of war, distance—and apparently—a distracted and unprotective husband. By the time David and his wife were finally reunited, Michal's love for him had withered away. Her last appearance in Scripture is a bitter confrontation with David over his "undignified" religious dancing on a day of national celebration.

Abigail, Country Estate Owner—
Wife of David's Wilderness Years
(1 Samuel 25).

David meets Abigail during a low point of his life. King Saul has forcibly given Michal to another man and has put his former son-in-law on the nation's "most wanted" list. David and his men have spent years hiding out in the caves and deserts of southern Judah.

When a wealthy landowner named Nabal refuses to help out David's starving men—and adds a string of insults besides—David loses his temper and decides to attack the man's estate.

But Abigail, Nabal's wife, intervenes. She puts together a caravan-load of supplies and sets off to deliver them in person. When she meets David, she bows at his feet, begging him to blame her for the mean behavior of her husband. Then she delivers an inspiring message to David, reminding him that he is still the Lord's annointed, and that he'll be king one day. David comes to his senses and turns from his plan.

Within days Abigail's husband is dead, and after the period of mourning is over, David claims this remarkable woman for his own wife. As the loyal wife of God's outlaw, and later of God's anointed king, Abigail builds a legacy as the noblest of his wives.

Bathsheba, Stolen War Bride— Wife of David's Mid-Life Crisis
(2 Samuel 11, 12; 1 Kings 1, 2)

Even though God calls David "the man after his own heart," David's heart led him into a lot of trouble. The story of Bathsheba and David is a favorite of romance novelists and filmmakers, but like the story of Samson and Delilah, it's really more about weakness and lust than it is about love.

After David commits adultery with Bathsheba, he arranges the murder of her husband to cover up her pregnancy. Their scandalous secret is exposed when the prophet Nathan confronts David with his sin and tells the king that Bathsheba's child will die.

The hard reality of his sin sends David into deep remorse and repentance. He fasts and prays for the life of the baby. During this painful time, he pens the Bible's best-known prayer of repentance, Psalm 51.

Have mercy on me, O God,
   according to your unfailing love;
according to your great compassion
   blot out my transgressions.
For I know my transgressions,
   and my sin is always before me (verses 1,3).

But the baby dies as predicted. When another son is born, the couple names him Solomon, "peace." In one of the Bible's most touching scenes of restoration, Nathan reappears telling the new parents that God's name for Solomon is Jedidiah, "loved by the Lord."

As David ages, Bathsheba takes her place at the center of court business and is clearly the Queen Mother. Eventually, her son Solomon succeeds David as king.

In his failures with Bathsheba, David discovered the darkness of his own heart. He also came to see that the love relationship that mattered most to him was the one between himself and his God.

Whole books have been written on David's journey of the heart. Here we'll give you some practical pointers you may have never thought of, like, "Best not to marry a woman whose daddy wants to kill you." We'll also look at some questions that strike at the heart of everyday married life, like:

- What does it take to stay in love when life conspires against you?

- How can we help each other stay true to our life goals?

- Why are painful falls in marriage only a stumble away, and what can we do to keep on our feet?

David's greatest achievement in life was not those accomplishments recorded in the history books or even the stunning inner qualities that shine through in Michelangelo's art. He was, most impressive of all, a friend of God. Even with all his failures, God boasted about him later as ". . . my servant David, who kept my commands and followed me with all his heart . . ." (1 Kings 14:8).

And for our benefit, God gave us more insight into David's performance as a husband than any other spouse's in Scripture. It's as if God is saying to every married person, "Come close. Listen to this tattered, lovely heart. Learn from the best."

As the ark of the LORD was entering the City of David, Michal daughter of Saul watched from a window. And when she saw King David leaping and dancing before the LORD, she despised him in her heart."

—2 SAMUEL 6:16

1 A Fragile Trust

Although David's ascent to the throne is at the center of this drama, the love story really belongs to Michal. All indications are that Michal's love for David was sincere. Scripture tells us *twice* that Michal loved David. And when forced to choose between loyalty to her father and love for her husband, Michal chose David, saving his life in the process.

So how is it that her story opens with the words, "Now Saul's daughter Michal was in love with David . . ." (1 Samuel 18:20) but ends with, "she despised him in her heart"? How did such devotion deteriorate into hatred?

Much of Michal's story turns on events that seem beyond her control: betrayal, abandonment, separation. We're not surprised that Michal becomes bitter. On the other hand, we've all watched relationships endure and even thrive in spite of awful hardships like scheming in-laws, long separations, and the death of loved ones. We discover sooner or later that the real enemy of a marriage isn't "out there," but inside—hiding in our own choices and attitudes.

Could Michal have chosen to keep loving? It's hard to keep a tender heart when you've been hurt deeply, but from Michal's mistakes and losses we can learn some preventative measures.

Don't harbor unforgiveness. Michal's anger when she saw David dancing before the ark didn't spring from jealousy, as much as from a long-standing bitterness. Paul reminds us to "see to it that no one misses the grace of God and that no bitter root grows up to cause trouble . . ." (Hebrews 12:15).

Don't be a victim. Maybe you, like Michal, have been victimized by a spouse or even a parent. That doesn't mean that you have to continue to live as a victim. Instead, look for ways to affect your circumstances instead of being controlled by them. As Merle Shain writes, "There are only two ways to approach life—as a victim or as a gallant fighter. You must decide if you want to act or react."

Don't be defined by your past. Like her father before her, Michal grew to hate David. And like her father, she became miserable and bitter. When we fail to reconcile with our past disappointments or injuries, we tend to repeat the patterns that led to them in the first place. God promises us that we can let go of the past and move on to better things (Isaiah 43:18-19).

Imagine a different final scene at the window: Michal has forgiven her tortured, abusive father. She sees how, partly through her own extreme sacrifice, God has protected and exalted her husband—and through him, her nation. When she looks down at her husband dancing in the streets, she remembers not a series of injustices, but a young man who brought music and laughter into a lonely palace long ago.

Yes, love is a fragile trust. And when it is broken, we hurt. But with God's help, we can guard against bitterness and reach instead for healing.

Forgiving Father,

Thank You for Your promise that we can put the past behind us and go forward to better things. Show us where unforgiveness might be holding us prisoner, where an ongoing conflict needs healthy closure, or where we can take brave, hard steps toward change. Amen.

Love Talk

What does it mean to behave like a victim in marriage? Sometimes it can be easier to spot this in another's marriage. Start there, then explore the issue in your own relationship.

2 Love Intervention

The scene is a hot and desolate ravine in southern Judah. A woman rides a donkey up the dry stream bed, followed at a distance by a caravan of pack animals straining under loads of food, fruits, and wine.

Suddenly armed marauders appear, dozens of them, surging over the rim ahead and careening down the slopes toward the woman. The men are sun-blackened, armed to the teeth, and shouting mad.

The woman dismounts. When the fighters are only paces away, they stop. But their leader keeps advancing, bellowing through the dust, ". . . Be it ever so severely, if by morning I leave alive one male of all who belong to him!"

The woman bows nearly to the ground. The man stops his ranting. Then halts.

"My Lord," she says in the sudden silence.

Not the place you'd expect to meet an attractive, young, and obviously well-to-do woman, which is what David did as soon as Abigail stood up. The Bible describes her as "intelligent and beautiful." And the famed desert warrior was on his way to murder her husband and her entire household.

151

David's life up to now had included many encounters with enormous obstacles. Goliath, for example. The Philistine armies. A murderous King Saul. But Abigail was the best and prettiest obstacle of his life. And when she stopped David in his tracks with the truth about who he was, she won his respect as well as his heart.

Can you remember a time recently when you or your spouse have felt especially under siege? In an emotional desert? On the verge of doing something really stupid? At such times, we need each other to be wise obstacles and loving interveners. We could learn a lot from Abigail:

Affirm your mate's integrity: Abigail reminded David that he was only the warrior; the battle belonged to the Lord. She counseled him against compromise. "Let no wrongdoing be found in you," she urged (verse 28).

Affirm your mate's calling and destiny: Abigail reminded David of his life purpose—"the LORD will certainly make a lasting dynasty for my master" (verse 28).

Affirm God's faithfulness: Abigail reminded David that God could be trusted, even when circumstances looked terrible— "The life of my master will be bound securely in the bundle of the living by the LORD your God" (verse 29).

Affirm your mate's future success: Abigail referred to the when, not if, of eventual success. You *will* get there if you hold on. "When the LORD has brought my master success, remember your servant" (verse 31).

By then it's likely David was thinking, "How could I forget a woman like you?" When we're in danger of losing our way, we need to hear the truth about who we are and who we're meant to be. This is one of love's most beautiful and unforgettable gifts.

Lord,

Help me to recognize the gifts of the God-anointed person I live with, a chosen being celebrated by You and called to a special purpose. And when my partner loses sight of this truth, let me be the beautiful intervener, holding out Your words of wisdom and encouragement. Amen.

Read 1 Samuel 25 aloud together. Talk about how it would feel to give, and to receive, Abigail's speech in your marriage.

One evening David got up from his bed and walked around on the roof of the palace. From the roof he saw a woman bathing. The woman was very beautiful, and David sent someone to find out about her. The man said, "Isn't this Bathsheba, . . . the wife of Uriah the Hittite?" Then David sent messengers to get her.
—2 Samuel 11:2-4

3 A Worm in the Heart

Twenty years had passed since David's days as a fugitive. Now he had a secure kingdom, a large royal family, and—unfortunately, as it turned out—time on his hands. Time to get into trouble with a bathing beauty named Bathsheba.

What was he thinking? A businessman might accuse David of an arsonist management style. That's where a company leader continually puts his operation at risk because he thrives on the challenge of rescuing it. Voters could compare King David to President Clinton—taking outrageous sexual risks that could compromise his authority and demean his office.

Think about the tabloid headlines:

"Bathsheba Bares All for Palace Viewing"

"The King's Fling: What Did He Know & When Did He Know It?"

"Confirmed: Soldier's Sweetheart Royally Pregnant!"

But what was the real news here? Something much less sensational—maybe, "King Suffers from Ailing Heart." After a lifetime of fidelity, a worm had worked its way into David's beautiful love affair with God. Not one of us can say this lightly or judgmentally. In our own lives, moral failure is always just a wiggle away.

When Nathan confronted King David with his sin and the cover-up (2 Samuel 11-12), he expresses God's grief over the matter. "This is what the LORD, God of Israel, says: 'I anointed you king over Israel, and I delivered you from the hand of Saul. I gave your master's house to you, and your master's wives into your arms. I gave you the house of Israel and Judah. And if all this had been too little, I would have given you even more'" (2 Samuel 12:7-8).

Such agony and rage. Anyone who's experienced a complete break in trust can understand God's feelings. Someone has said, "He who sins against love sins against himself." But David knew that for believers, it goes even deeper. In Psalm 51, he poured out his repentance: "Against you, you only, have I sinned and done what is evil in your sight." Then later he pleads, "Do not cast me from your presence" (verses 4,11).

In this tragedy we recognize several hard truths about ourselves:

- None of us is exempt from temptation (maybe *especially* when everything seems to be going well).

- Sin always brings consequences.

- Sexual sin always breaks hearts—ours, our mates', and our God's.

No past success or present comfort can keep us safe from the fallenness of our nature. As David wrote, "Surely I was sinful . . . from the time my mother conceived me" (verse 5). But a humble daily surrender to God's indwelling Spirit is the place to start.

Lord,

*I pray with David today: "Create in me a pure heart,
O God, and renew a steadfast spirit within me. Do not
cast me from your presence or take your Holy Spirit
from me" (Psalm 51:10-11).*

David's son, Solomon, also sinned against love and ag-
onized over its effects. Read his advice in Proverbs
4:23: "Guard your heart, for it is the wellspring of
life." How will you guard your hearts together?

Praise the LORD, O my soul, and forget not all his benefits—who forgives all your sins and hails all your diseases, who redeems your life from the pit and crowns you with love and compassion.

— DAVID (PSALM 103:2-3)

4 All the King's Wives

While David reigned as king he had at least eight wives we know of. In addition to Michal, Abigail, and Bathsheba, there were Ahinoam, Maacha, Haggith, Abital, and Eglah (1 Chronicles 3:1-9).

When the time came for David to anoint his successor, Bathsheba and Haggith battled over whose son would succeed him (1 Kings 1:11-12). But what of the famous three? Did Abigail keep to herself, choosing to sidestep both the haughty has-been princess Michal and the young, ravishing Bathsheba? Did they ever argue like Rachel and Leah or Peninnah and Hannah?

If only we could get the three in the same room for an interview with Barbara Walters. Better yet, if we could eavesdrop on a hot afternoon while the women lounged by the palace pool. It might go something like this:

> "I hear you're maneuvering for your son to be king, Bathsheba," Michal drawls as she slaps more scented oil on her tummy. "It's not enough that you're a king's wife when you should have been stoned for adultery. Now you expect your descendants to rule?"
>
> "How dare you!" exclaims Bathsheba.

"No offense," pipes Michal. "But it just seems like it's worked out pretty well for you. You got rid of your husband—"

"Listen here," Bathsheba interrupts. "I loved Uriah. He was a man of honor. I was heartsick when he was murdered. But then, what would you know of love, Michal? Much less of sons?"

"Oh, come now, Bath," Michal replies coolly. "Honor? Face it—you were just another war widow. Uriah didn't even think about the fact that you might be needing some wifely attentions. Or that you'd end up so quickly in another man's bed, and the king's bed at that!"

Abigail, who has been sunning quietly next to Michal, rolls over now and murmurs, "Come now, Michal. Is this really necessary? It's beautiful out. We are all the king's wives. And our separate sorrows have made us all, well, sisters . . ."

All three of David's wives came to him through extraordinary circumstances, and each faced hardships in her role as wife. Michal was once traded to another husband, and was barren. Abigail had been married to an evil brute. Bathsheba had been publicly exposed in adultery and lost her first son as a judgment for her sin.

David's love stories, like many of ours, were anything but neat and tidy. Yet God used even these negative circumstances to further his purposes in David's life. For example: He used Michal, intended by her father to be a snare to David, to save David's life. He used Abigail's awful husband to bring her to the desert to encourage and affirm David. And from Bathsheba's marriage, which began in adultery, God brought Solomon—the future king—and some of the most cherished writings in Scripture.

Does your marriage seem too full of trouble and heartache to make sense? Join David in declaring: "The LORD will fulfill his purpose for me [and my spouse]. Your love, O LORD, endures forever—do not abandon the works of your hands" (Psalm 138:8).

Lord,

How I thank You for bringing my mate and I together for Your purposes, that together we might seek Your strength. Together may we bring honor to Your name. Together may we offer You thanks! Amen.

 What negative circumstance has God used for good in your marriage?

You have made known to me the path of life;
you will fill me with joy in your presence, with
eternal pleasures at your right hand.
                              —David (PSALM 16:11)

5 The Greatest Love Affair

When you've finished reading the entire saga of David—his adventures, heroics, and especially his psalms—the love stories involving his wives begin to recede into the background. You might note, for example, that the Bible hardly mentions David's feelings about the women he married. Nowhere do we read, "But David loved Michal" or "David fell in love with the wise and beautiful Abigail."

Instead, when David poured out his heart, exulted, and overflowed with passion, the object of his affection was not a woman at all. It was God.

Consider this fact: The turning points with David's wives really boiled down to turning points in David's relationship with God. When Michal's bitterness finally erupts at David over his unselfconscious dancing before the ark, he makes a choice, and it's not for Michal's approval either: "I will celebrate before the Lord. I will become even more undignified than this. . . ." (2 Samuel 6:21-22). After his adultery, David cries out to God, "Against you, you only, have I sinned" and "Do not cast me from your presence" (Psalm 51:4,11). But we don't know what, if anything, he said to Bathsheba.

Should we assume that David wasn't sorry for sinning against Bathsheba and Uriah, or that his marriages didn't matter to him? No. But his actions illustrate David's lifelong first love. Consider some of his "love notes" to his Maker, taken from the psalms (hint: If they ring a bell, you're probably thinking of the Song of Songs):

> "Keep me as the apple of your eye" (17:8).
>
> "I love you, O LORD, my strength" (18:1).
>
> "When I awake, I will be satisfied with seeing your likeness" (17:15).
>
> "How precious to me are your thoughts, O God!" (139:17).
>
> "Let the morning bring me word of your unfailing love" (143:8).

Too often we have a natural tendency to seek from our spouse what only God can give us—life, happiness, peace, and joy. Our "significant relationship" has become a sort of god in our culture. We expect a spouse to satisfy all our needs, take away all our loneliness, and comfort us in all our uncertainties. God gets whatever is left over in terms of our affections and time.

In the long run, most marriages don't bear up very well under such pressure. A spouse simply can't make everything all right. When a woman hangs all her hopes on her husband to fill up her empty heart, she's headed for disappointment. Likewise, a man's wife—though a beautiful and wondrous gift—was never intended to be worshiped.

David had the right idea. The best marriage is made up of two people whose first love relationship is with God. Then each, knowing he or she is "the apple of God's eye," can come to the other not as a needy, greedy spouse, but overflowing with still more love (Philippians 1:9).

Lover of My Soul,

Thank You for giving me my flesh-and-blood spouse. But I also want to know what it means to cherish You first and most. Forgive me for the times I turn to my mate with needs and concerns that only You can meet—and that You stand ready and able to meet. Remind us all day today that You long to lavish Your love on us (1 John 3:1). Amen.

 Are there needs or demands you make on each other that would be better taken to the Lord? And what would it mean to put God first today?

CHAPTER NINE

The Lover & The Beloved

About the Lover

Name: Identified only as the "Lover" in the NIV;
traditionally assumed to be Solomon as a young prince

Age at Marriage: Unknown, possibly 18-25

Appearance: Handsome and charming, according to
his "Beloved"

Family Background: Presented as being from Jerusalem
(Solomon was King David's son by Bathsheba; he became
king of Israel in 971 B.C.

Place in History: As the "Lover," he is the handsome
suitor from the royal court who woos a beautiful
country girl

About the Beloved

Name: Identified as the Shulamite or Shunammite,
she was a shepherd girl from the town of Shunem. Since
there is no other name, the NIV identifies her in the notes
as "Beloved"

Age at Marriage: Probably a teenager

Appearance: By her own description, "dark am I, yet lovely"

Family Background: She is presented as a country girl

Place in History: The young woman who both evokes
and speaks the Bible's most inspired love poetry

Celebrating the Pursuit of Intimacy

Song of Songs

You wander upstairs to your grandparents' attic. They've recently passed on, but you sense their presence here amid the hatboxes, wooden skis, and wardrobes. When you find a trunk full of papers, you sit down to browse.

Before long the written record of a lifetime spent together is spread out before you: postcards, birth certificates, notarized documents, awards, yellowed news clippings, photos. Your eye lands on a cedar jewelry box and you open it to discover not earrings, but love letters.

In spite of yourself, you start reading. Phrases jump out at you, like *"You are so beautiful, my darling"* and *"You stole my heart with one glance of your eyes."* When you stumble onto *"Your breasts are like . . . ,"* you stop. Whew! You had no idea. Two sweet, staid, ordinary people. But, my, what a love affair they had!

The Song of Songs falls into our laps like those letters. In the middle of God's anthology of histories and biographies and teachings, out tumbles a packet of love letters. They tell about sexual intimacies—*"let him kiss me with the kisses of his mouth."* And playfulness—*"Come, my lover, let us go to the countryside, let us spend the night in the villages—there I will give you my love."* And confessions shared among friends—*"If you find my lover, tell him I am faint with love."*

The Song of Songs (meaning the *greatest* of songs) is presumed to have been written by King Solomon. It has to be the most unusual book in the Bible. Consider: It dwells on perfume and lips and hair, but doesn't mention God or give any theological or moral teachings. It records the dreamy thoughts of a pair of smitten Jewish lovers, but never once refers to any history or laws or prophecy about the Jewish nation.

And the storyline is, well, a swoony blur. Is it about the young King Solomon and his bride? Or about a shepherdess and a shepherd? Some commentators even find three characters here—a shepherd and a king both pursuing a shepherdess, who remains true to her shepherd lover. Many enjoy the New International Version's simplified presentation. It presents the poem like a Greek drama with two characters—a lover, a beloved—and a chorus that echoes or comments on the action.

Let the experts debate—this packet of love letters has been a Bible favorite for generations, no matter the questions. For example, the Songs are read aloud every Passover in synagogues around the world. Jews treasure it as a statement of God's enduring love for His people. And Christians see the book as an allegory of Christ the Heavenly Bridegroom's love for His bride, the church. It's been a favorite of mystics, poets, girls just discovering young love, and boys looking for something to smirk at in church.

But the book really belongs to husbands and wives. For us, it shines like a diamond of committed love set into the gold of Scripture. It gives us words for the yearnings that bind us together. And it declares to our careless, selfish, and debased world, *"Love and romance and sex are God's living gifts, and marriage is where they blossom best!"*

Even though the Songs is not a teaching book, we can find plenty of love lessons to take into our bedrooms—insights about maintaining intimacy, the importance of pursuit in a romantic relationship, the delights of pure sexual passion, and the mysterious power of words to make our hearts beat faster.

Taken as a whole, the book tries to describe the nature and meaning of human romantic love. It presents us with this paradox: "Love is about feelings" and "Love is not about feelings." This makes sense. We all know that to worship the feelings alone, apart from commitment, can as easily get us into an extramarital affair as into a marriage.

These love letters chronicle almost every emotion of romance—separation and intimacy, anguish and bliss, longing and contentment. But they go beyond feelings to paint a clear picture of what godly love is meant to be. For example, a great love relationship (as God intended it to be) is:

- Exclusive: "My lover is mine and I am his" (2:16).

- Pure: "You are a garden locked up, my sister, my bride; you are a spring enclosed, a sealed fountain" (4:12).

- Patient: "Do not arouse or awaken love until it so desires" (2:7).

- Powerful: "love is as strong as death, its jealousy as unyielding as the grave" (8:6).

- Enduring: "Many waters cannot quench love; rivers cannot wash it away" (8:7).

- Priceless: "If one were to give all the wealth of his house for love, it would be utterly scorned" (8:7).

Interestingly, when we've finished the one book in the Bible that is entirely about romantic love, we realize we've never been told the couple's names. We've entered their most intimate reveries and heard their voices (or perused their mail), but never actually met them.

Why? Maybe God meant for each of us to personalize the Song, making it our own love letter to the one we love, and receiving it in the same way. Perhaps He wanted to make sure we'd never be struck dumb when words mattered most, that husbands and wives would always have line upon line of new ways to say, "Be mine!"

Your lips are like a scarlet ribbon; your
mouth is lovely. . . . How beautiful you are and
how pleasing, O love, with your delights!
—SONG OF SONGS 4:3; 7:6

1 In Praise of Kisses

So if God is a spirit, how did He figure out what it would take to really enjoy having a body? If you were color-blind and the whole universe came in shades of black and white, could you have thought up lime green? Can a rock imagine a string quartet?

But think about this: God intricately designed us to experience whole-body and whole-heart sexual pleasure. He made lips for kissing and smooth skin for caressing and soft eyelashes for fluttering. He made the wondrous female form, not as an exercise in design or pure function, but as an expression of delight. *"Here she is, Adam,"* He said. *"Isn't she something?"*

And into the woman God breathed a desire for her husband, and in him God made a circuit with all wires leading to a switch marked *"Her."* And then God flipped the switch on—permanently.

Procreation wasn't really the issue, you know. God could have signed us up for simple division, like amoebas, or remote multiplication, like turtles making their deposits in the sand.

But God thought human sexuality was a great idea. He loved the idea of man and wife in a long embrace. He actually wanted pounding hearts and quickened breath. And in case we didn't get the picture, He threw in about a million extra nerve endings in certain places, direct-feed hormone pumps, and eyes and fingers custom-made for sensory input. And in case that still wasn't enough, He gave us technicolor imaginations.

Sex and romance were God's idea—and He put a whole book in the Bible to prove it. But why might it have been so important to make this sensuous love poem part of Scripture?

For one thing, that God should have set the Song of Songs in the middle of the Scriptures tells us how important lovemaking is between husband and wife. The lover says, "Your two breasts are like two fawns . . . that browse among the lilies" (4:5). The beloved answers, "I am my lover's and my lover is mine; he browses among the lilies" (6:3).

This beautiful coming together that we call sex is about more than pleasure or even making children. The urgency and necessity of physical oneness over a lifetime reminds us that our hearts and our bodies are one being. Our world keeps trying to separate the two, and put each up for sale. But God's idea (since Eden) has always been that love deepens sex, and sex deepens love—and marriage creates a setting for the enjoyment of each that can't be duplicated.

Most of us look nothing like the perfectly proportioned, eternally young people who occupy the screens and pages of our world. But God's imagination for the human race was much more interesting (and possible) than that! Whatever our age or physical appearance, God meant for our bodies to be a gift of continuing delight—to our hearts and to our mates.

Lord of Lips and Breasts and Shoulders and Fingertips,
  Be Lord of my body today. Be Lord of my imagination,
and of my heart. Let my lover and I sing our Song of
Songs to You today out of pure joy and appreciation and
worship. Thank You for Your lavish gifts. Amen.

 How could you appreciate and enjoy each other physically in a new way today?

My dove in the clefts of the rock, in the
hiding places on the mountainside, show me
your face, let me hear your voice; for your voice
is sweet, and your face is lovely.
—SONG OF SONGS 2:14

2 The Great Pursuit

Have you noticed that the lovers in Songs are rarely depicted together? Their drama is less about the consummation of love than the zigzagging journey toward it. In one scene, they're in hot pursuit, inviting the other to "Come away with me." In the next, they're coy, reluctant to answer the door.

In chapter 3, the beloved can't find her lover even though she desperately searches. You can probably remember a similar experience: *Why isn't she answering the phone? Have I lost her?* Later you realized this was exactly what she had in mind.

Silly love games? Yes—and no. "That's the way we are made," explains James Dobson. "Most of us want what we have to stretch for—what we can only dream about achieving. We are excited by a challenge—by that which is mysterious and elusive."

Flowers and candlelight dinners are really just another way to say: "I want to catch you! You're worth trying to know and possess. I'll go to great lengths to impress you and win you!"

So how do we keep the pursuit alive?

This is one of the places where marriages often break down. One or both of us decide our spouse is now a known commodity, no longer a mystery to discover or a prize to win. Maybe one of us has made matters worse by smothering the other, giving him or her little incentive or room to pursue.

The longer we've been married, the more proficient we need to become at the art of pursuit and invitation. Ask: "How long has it been since I stepped back and noticed some new tender shoot trying to surface in my partner's soul?" Many affairs have their origin here—the marriage partner has simply stopped noticing. We'll nearly always find those new shoots if we look for them, and it's crucial that *we* be the one to explore it and delight in it with our partner.

We should also ask: "Am I making an effort to be a separate, growing person?" And "To get attention, do I tend to invite or smother?" Dobson advises: "Keep the mystery and dignity in your relationship. If the other partner begins to feel trapped and withdraws for a time, grant him or her some space and pull back yourself."

Today, consider some ideas for practical pursuing: genuine listening, follow-up questions, compliments, affirmations, asking for time together, thoughtful gifts, speaking well of him or her to others.

And some ideas for encouraging pursuit: paying attention to your appearance—dress, cleanliness, fitness, and grooming; responsiveness; special favors; eye contact and lingering touches; and sincere personal sharing.

The point is not to play games or to make one another insecure. We need not always be either in pursuit mode or in retreat. But each marriage needs to find a romantic rhythm that works, one where each person feels wanted and has the chance to want.

Lord of Romance,

Help us to pursue one another tenderly and persistently, like we did as new lovers, and like You pursue us every day. Thank You that each of us is a miracle in the making, a person always changing. Show us new ways to explore one another's souls and say, "I want you!" Amen.

 Take some time to talk about your patterns of pursuit and retreat. Are they obvious? Do they work?

I have taken off my robe—must I put it on again? I have washed my feet—must I soil them again?. . . I opened for my lover, but my lover had left; he was gone. My heart sank at his departure.

—SONG OF SONGS 5:3,6

3 In the Mood for Love

One of the most delightful aspects of the Song of Songs is that it covers so many aspects of the romantic experience; even ambivalence. In this passage, the woman is not rejecting her lover. After all, her heart sinks at his departure. But she's not "in the mood," having already gotten ready for bed. So she delays responding, and the opportunity for intimacy is lost.

Sound familiar? Most of us experience occasions when the timing of our desire for intimacy, particularly lovemaking, doesn't match our mate's. Our lover approaches with passion in his or her eyes and we feel inconvenienced or just plain tired. Or maybe we're the one who wants to make love and feels rejected if our mate says, "Not tonight, honey."

What does the Bible have to say about this dilemma? Paul reminds us that "the husband should fulfill his marital duty to his wife, and likewise the wife to her husband. The wife's body does not belong to her alone but also to her husband. In the same way, the husband's body does not belong to him alone but also to his wife" (1 Corinthians 7:3-4).

Notice that Paul didn't say your body belongs *only* to your spouse, but *also* to your spouse. As "one flesh" we *share* our body with our mate. But this doesn't mean we get to be inconsiderate when it comes to lovemaking. Just the opposite. If my mate's body belongs to me, I should be willing to forgo my satisfaction for a time—or likewise, make an effort to receive and respond to my partner's advances.

Wouldn't it be nice if we were always in the mood together, equally passionate and interested at the same time? Instead, lovemaking requires thought, care, and sometimes even work. When moods or timing just don't match, however, here are some ways you can keep from misunderstandings or hurt:

- *Reassure your mate of his or her desirability:* A husband who knows by his wife's words, touches, and looks that she finds him desirable is less likely to take a "no" personally.

- *Be honest about your feelings:* A wife who only pretends to want or enjoy a sexual encounter isn't doing herself or her husband a favor. Communication is key to lovemaking. Tell each other the truth—in love—about everything.

- *Prepare for lovemaking all day:* The best way to be in the mood together is to *get* in the mood together. When you invite your spouse at breakfast to an interlude after dinner, you can build on good feelings all day long.

In all these things, keep in mind your goal—that both of you be able to say with satisfaction, "I belong to my lover, and his desire is for me" (7:10).

Lord of Love,

Today I pray that You would help me to be sensitive to my mate's sexual advances. Let me welcome them with gladness. And when I'm not able—physically or emotionally—to make love, help me to remember how vulnerable my spouse is at these moments. Help us both to be patient when one of us must wait for passion to awaken in the other. Amen.

Talk with your partner about your similarities and differences in regard to desire for sex. How can you become more sensitive to the other?

How beautiful you are, my darling! Oh, how
beautiful! Your eyes are like doves.
How handsome you are, my lover! Oh, how
charming.

—Song of Songs 1:15-16

4 Love Talk

Throughout Song of Songs, the lovers delight in exchanging compliments and invitations to love. Each is anxious to be told how the other feels. Both talk constantly about each other's bodies, hands, lips, hair, and voices, and about their longings for each other.

If pursuit is at the heart of romance, then words of love are how we give chase. Like casting a love-net over our beloved, our lavish praises have the power to capture the heart of our mate. She feels completely known, seen, and appreciated—as if no beautiful part of her being has gone undiscovered. He feels admired and desired.

You can tell by the language of the Song that both lover and beloved were familiar with nature and country living. For us, phrases such as "your teeth are like a flock of sheep" and "your waist is a mound of wheat" will most likely only get a blank look, or worse.

What kind of love talk would set off sparks for us? The example of the couple in Song of Songs reveals several useful suggestions:

Use language that resonates with your lover: The lovers in Songs used sensuous references from their world—spices, gardens, perfume, sweet fruits—to communicate love in a way the other would understand. What kinds of words have the most effect on your spouse? Does poetry thrill her? Does he prefer playful come-ons in his ear? Does she like written sentiments so she can savor them longer? Would he prefer a CD of love songs?

Repeat your praises frequently: The lover in Song of Songs tells his beloved six times that she's beautiful. You've probably heard of the man who boasted, "I never repeat myself. I told my wife I loved her when we got married and if anything changes, I'll let her know." Not many would envy his wife. Most of us need ongoing reassurances of our mate's love and admiration. As P.T. Forsyth says, "Love loves to be told what it knows already. It wants to be asked for what it longs to give."

Be creative and spontaneous: In an effort to repeat our praises, it's so easy to lapse into tired patterns. When we're specific and thoughtful—"I love the way you look in a suit"—our spouse knows we're really paying attention. Instead of saying, "You look nice, honey," try something like, "I love the way your blue eyes look when you wear that blue dress."

Be sincere and authentic: The picture we have of love in the Song of Songs is the opposite of empty flattery. It is a sincere, heartfelt expression that isn't offered dutifully or as a manipulative gesture. The lovers here are exchanging genuine affection and admiration.

Today, think of three ways to praise your spouse, using descriptive phrases that you've never used before. Think of every compliment as trying to answer the question put to the woman by her friends: *How is your beloved better than others?*

Author of Love,

Your Word tells me that even a rebuke is better than unspoken love (Proverbs 27:5). Help me today to use the beautiful gift of words to seduce my spouse, compliment my spouse, praise my spouse. And may my words bring joy, security, and healing. Amen.

 Share what kinds of compliments mean the most to you, and why.

Place me like a seal over your heart, like a seal on your arm; for love is as strong as death, its jealousy unyielding as the grave. It burns like blazing fire, like a mighty flame. Many waters cannot quench love; rivers cannot wash it away. If one were to give all the wealth of his house for love, it would be utterly scorned.

—SONG OF SONGS 8:6-7

5 *Many Waters*

Commentators agree that this passage is the literary climax of the Song of Songs. All the feelings, conversations, and physical descriptions that have come before make the case for love. Now comes the conclusion: Love is incredibly strong and enduring, and it can't be bought at any price.

Most of us tend to think of love as intense feelings—what the poet Theodore Roethke calls "the weather of heaven." And feelings certainly swirl through the Song of Songs, first one way, then another. But by the end of the book, the author wants to be sure we know what all the storms and heat waves have been about. Genuine love, the author asserts, is power. In just a few verses, the beloved delivers four memorable statements about love:

- *"Place me like a seal over your heart. . ."* In Bible times, a seal was a personal guarantee. It indicated a direct link between the person and any document on which it was placed. Here, the woman asks her lover to give her permanent ownership of his heart.

- *"For love is as strong as death, its jealousy as unyielding as the grave."* The finality of death gives a picture of the uncompromising bonds of love. Just as the grave

181

won't surrender the dead, a lover refuses to give up his or her beloved. The jealousy mentioned here isn't peevishness or insecurity, but our fierce instinct to guard and set ownership boundaries around our beloved.

- *"It burns like . . . a mighty flame . . . Many waters cannot quench love."* Water would normally extinguish a flame. But this juxtaposition of water and fire depicts love as so powerful that it defies the laws of nature. It's ability to overcome life's obstacles is mysterious, unexplainable, and wonderful.

- *"If one were to give all the wealth of his house for love, it would be utterly scorned."* Love is priceless. We know we can't buy it, and we'd consider anyone who actually tried a certified fool.

Love that is permanent, exclusive, unquenchable, and priceless—isn't that the kind of love we all want in our marriages and families? Isn't the hope of building it why you're reading this book?

Many couples conclude that these qualities are at best only ideals, at worst outrageous claims for what love can do (just ask any divorce attorney, they say). It's true that many waters do flood into our marriages. Someone has to take out the garbage, cook, battle traffic, get up at 3 A.M. to change the baby. Her driving makes him want to walk. His behavior at parties makes her want to hide.

Can love be unquenchable here, too? The promise of the Bible is simple—"Yes." And hard—"But you have to choose it."

Did you notice? This hymn to the true nature of love isn't really about feelings. Instead, these verses declare the realistic potential and power of love. God made us to want it, reach for it, and—with His help—be capable of it. But genuine, redeeming love always requires a decision, sometimes a painful one.

Paul calls this the "most excellent way" that "never fails" (1 Corinthians 13:1,8).

Dear Father,

Teach me about love's amazing power. Help me choose it today, and see its power at work. You know the waters we face together. Amen.

Practice floating over threatening waters today. You "float" when you say, "Honey, this situation makes me anxious and crabby, but I still love you. I'm glad we're together." Identify a trial or daily irritation you face, label it for what it is, and then keep it from flooding your marriage.

CHAPTER TEN

Hosea & Gomer

About Hosea

Name: Means "deliverance"
Age at Marriage: Unknown
Appearance: Unknown
Personality: Sensitive, compassionate, determined, committed
Family Background: Son of Beeri, an upper-class family in the northern kingdom of Israel
Place in History: The prophet God ordered to marry an unfaithful wife as a living demonstration of how God felt about Israel's idolatry

About Gomer

Name: Means "complete"
Age at Marriage: Probably early twenties
Appearance: Unknown, presumably attractive
Personality: Probably vivacious and bold
Family Background: Her father, Diblaim, worshiped Baal
Place in History: The prostitute who became the wife of the prophet Hosea

Reaching for Forgiveness

Hosea 1–3, 14

Imagine yourself on the streets of Samaria, the capital city of Israel during the days of the Northern Kingdom. Samaria is a bustling, prosperous city of handsome buildings and winding streets. Roses trail over garden walls. In the marketplace, traders hawk their wares from crowded stalls.

And on a street corner, right across from the temple of Baal, stands a man shouting.

His name is Hosea, a prophet of God. Pigeons flap around his head. Strangers spit in his direction. But Hosea doesn't seem to notice. He preaches on, and every word is about God's broken heart.

As you watch Hosea, you notice a woman walk up. Obviously, they're familiar with each other. The preacher breaks off in mid-sentence to listen. The woman (could she be a prostitute?) delivers a message defiantly. She wears no veil and offers no courtesies as she waves her bangled arms in his face. As she spins around to leave, Hosea reaches for her. But she shrugs him off and fades into the crowd.

Hosea stands silently, looking in the direction his wife has gone . . . You've just met the Bible's most remarkable married couple—Hosea and Gomer. This week, it seems, things are not going well for them. Again.

The book of Hosea is mostly a collection of prophetic messages directed toward the Northern Kingdom (called Samaria, Ephraim, or Israel in the book). They come at a time (about 750 B.C.) when the nation is being threatened by Assyria, a superpower from the east. God wants His people to know that judgment will come if they don't return to righteous living. Hosea's messages use the picture of a love relationship between a husband and a wife: God is the loving husband; Israel is the straying wife. By worshiping idols, she has betrayed her first love—and His heart is broken.

But there is an even more dramatic element in the story: God asks Hosea to show Israel how he feels by means of a living demonstration. "Take a prostitute as your wife," He tells Hosea. "And when she runs after other men, keep showing her your love." Hosea's mission, then, was not just to preach *about* God's feelings, but to *feel them, live them, suffer them.* Ultimately, Hosea demonstrated the kind of radical forgiveness that would eventually become available in Christ—and that we are each called to extend to each other.

The autobiographical part of the book is scattered through the first three chapters:

- Hosea takes Gomer as his wife, as God has instructed (1:2-3).

- They have three children together (with the distinct possibility that they are not all Hosea's) (1:4,6,9).

- Gomer proves unfaithful and leaves (strongly implied in 2:2-23).

- God asks Hosea to "go, show your love to your wife again, though she is loved by another and is an adulteress. Love her as the LORD loves the Israelites" (Hosea 3:1).

- Hosea proceeds to pay 15 shekels to "buy back" Gomer, who had apparently sold herself into a brothel (Hosea 3:2).

As we watch this couple live through one of the worst imaginable marriage stories, we see God Himself looking over their shoulders, weeping. Through Hosea He wails, "What can I do with you, Ephraim? Your love is like the morning mist, like the early dew that disappears" (Hosea 6:4).

But Hosea and Gomer's story is finally one of hope and encouragement. In their painful experiences, we see lived out the healing power of forgiveness in marriage and the radical love of God for each of us.

The LORD said to me, "Go, show your love to your wife again, though she is loved by another and is an adulteress."

—HOSEA 3:1

1 Early to Forgive

How many of us would take back, much less *show love* to, a straying husband or wife—especially one who wasn't even sorry?

The Bible doesn't tell us whether Gomer ever repented for her adulterous life. We don't know if she was grateful to be rescued from slavery by her husband. But God didn't ask Hosea to wait around for an apology or some sign of repentance from Gomer.

Today Hosea would probably be counseled to let his selfish, rebellious wife go her own way. "Who needs her? You deserve better than that. Even the Bible allows for divorce in cases of adultery. . . ."

And yet, even if Gomer *had* wanted to come home, her feelings of guilt and her estrangement from Hosea would probably have kept her away. Besides, she probably couldn't imagine that her prophet husband, devoted to righteous living, would take her back into his home again, much less love her.

But in doing just that, Hosea revealed God's heart toward Israel—and toward us. God pursues us and offers us His forgiveness even while we are running fast in the opposite direction.

Paul reminded the Romans of this when he wrote, "Or do you show contempt for the riches of his kindness, tolerance and patience, not realizing that God's kindness leads you toward repentance?" (Romans 2:4). And John declared rightly, "We love because he first loved us" (1 John 4:19).

So what does it mean to forgive our mate as Christ forgives (Colossians 3:13)? Christ forgives us freely. Quickly. Repeatedly. Without requirements. His forgiveness is unmerited. Undeserved. Often unrequested!

How hard it can be to offer this kind of forgiveness in marriage, especially after a heated or painful argument. Especially when we're convinced that our anger and hurt are legitimate and that we're in the right and our mate is in the wrong.

Yet sometimes it is only this kind of undeserved, aggressive forgiveness that has the power to break down the defenses of a stubborn heart. What if Hosea hadn't reached out to Gomer first? What if he hadn't shown her love in its truest form?

In fact, it's usually when we least deserve love and mercy that we most need to experience them from our mate. This is exactly what Christ demonstrated—"While we were still sinners, Christ died for us" (Romans 5:8). And it is this gift of undeserved forgiveness that, with Christ's help, we can offer our mates.

> *Jesus,*
> *Thank You for dying for us when we least deserved*
> *it! Please help us to grant this kind of forgiveness to*
> *each other. Some days it feels impossible. How greatly*
> *we need Your Spirit to work in us and in spite of us.*
> *Forgive us today, Lord, for being so slow to forgive when*
> *we have been forgiven so much. Amen.*

 Love Talk | Share with your mate your most powerful memory of being forgiven by him or her.

Then I told her, "You are to live with me
many days; you must not be a prostitute or
be intimate with any man, and I will live
with you."

—HOSEA 3:3

2 The Limits of Forgiveness

One of the reasons that many of us struggle to forgive is that
we misunderstand what it means. Not just in our head, but deep
in our soul. One common misunderstanding is to imagine that
when we forgive someone we are condoning, denying, or ignoring
their offense.

Take note that Hosea didn't say to Gomer, "It's just fine that
you did this to me. No problem." Instead, when he forgave Gomer
he also put his foot down and said, "You can't sleep with anyone
but me from now on!"

Even though Jesus forgave those who killed Him, this did not
negate the depth of their evil or the horror of what they had done
to Him. Their sin wasn't ignored. It was fully recognized, counted
as sin—and *forgiven!* And that is why His forgiveness was so
powerful.

Similarly, there are no limits on the forgiveness God asks us
to grant others or to expect for ourselves. But there are limits to
what forgiveness *means.* God didn't ask Hosea to bring his wife
home and allow her to continue to sin against their marriage
and do nothing about it. Just the opposite! He wanted to use this
relationship as a parable to show Israel how deeply compassionate

He felt toward them. But He also wanted Israel to return to Him *and become faithful.*

When Jesus encountered a woman like Gomer at a well in the same town some 500 years later, He forgave her, and then He told her, "Go now and leave your life of sin" (John 8:11).

A second misunderstanding about forgiveness involves our concept of how God approaches the issue. Many times we imagine a God who glosses over our wounds and pain. It's as if we're lying there bleeding and God comes by and says, "Hey, there. You look hurt. Did you forgive the guy who did that to you?"

No wonder we clutch our wounds so tightly.

But the truth is that God cares deeply about our wounds and He is angry on our behalf when others hurt us. The prophet Malachi explained to the Israelites why God was no longer accepting their offerings with pleasure. "You ask, 'Why?' It is because the LORD is acting as the witness between you and the wife of your youth, because you have broken faith with her, though she is your partner, the wife of your marriage covenant" (Malachi 2:14).

Yes, God asks us to forgive our mates over and over. But God is also our defender, the one who "acts as a witness" between us. And knowing this helps us to forgive our mate when they offend us, confident that we have a champion in heaven who cares.

> *Heavenly Father,*
> *Thank You for showing me the true face of forgiveness, reminding me that You are as concerned about me as You are about those You ask me to forgive. Please help me to keep choosing the path of compassion and grace-giving. May my spouse and I each act as each other's champion today, caring tenderly for the wounds we or others have inflicted. In Your precious name I pray. Amen.*

Share with your partner an incident or person from your past that you found hard to forgive—or still can't seem to forgive—and talk about why that may be.

I will betroth you to me forever; I will betroth
you in righteousness and justice, in love and
compassion. I will betroth you in faithfulness,
and you will acknowledge the LORD.
—HOSEA 2:19-20

3 A Faithful Heart

Nowhere else in the Bible does God so clearly compare our relationship with Him to a marriage as in the book of Hosea. But it is a marriage in which He is a jilted lover. The book overflows with tears, anger, and warnings, and God vascillates between wanting to punish and wanting to woo Israel.

But just as Gomer was a slave to a sinful life, Israel was enslaved by her sin. And though God begged and pleaded for her repentance, Israel did not turn back. "I long to redeem them," the Lord declared through Hosea, "but they speak lies against me. They do not cry out to me from their hearts . . ." (Hosea 7:13-14).

How can we guard against an unfaithful heart toward God or toward our mate?

Although it's impossible to know for sure what led Gomer into an adulterous life, it's easy to read the descriptions of harlotry in Hosea and think they sound too wicked or far-fetched to apply to us. A closer look, however, reveals that the essence of betrayal begins in our spirit—with arrogance, selfishness, stubbornness, and lust. God gives us many clues to the source of Israel's unfaithfulness in Hosea's prophecies:

- "A spirit of prostitution leads them astray; they are unfaithful to their God" (4:12).

- "Israel's arrogance testifies against them . . ." (5:5).

- "The Israelites are stubborn, like a stubborn heifer" (4:16).

Today, God still pleads with us through His spirit and the Scriptures to have faithful hearts. The promise Hosea spoke so long ago is still true: "In that day, declares the LORD, you will call me, 'my husband'" (2:16).

And guess what? Keeping a faithful heart toward God is the best defense against an adulterous heart in marriage. Both take effort and require a choice. The urgent words Hosea spoke centuries ago are still words for married lovers everywhere to say together. "Let us acknowledge the LORD; let us press on to acknowledge him. As surely as the sun rises, he will appear; he will come to us like the winter rains, like the spring rains that water the earth" (Hosea 6:3).

> Lord of Married Lovers,
>   I want to be faithful in every way—in body, emotions, mind, spirit, and imagination—to the spouse You have given me. You have said, "Marriage should be honored by all, and the marriage bed kept pure" (Hebrews 13:4). Show me anything in my life today that threatens the refreshing purity You want for me. Help me to be true in all I do. Amen.

Love Talk

Behind straying thoughts usually lie other root problems: pride, stubbornness, selfishness, refusal to delay gratification. Make two personal inventories: one of how these root problems might be affecting your relationship with God, the other of how they might be affecting your relationship with your spouse. Ask God to show you what changes you need to make.

Take words with you and return to the LORD.
Say to him: "Forgive all our sins and receive us
graciously, that we may offer the fruit of our
lips. Assyria cannot save us; we will not mount
war-horses. We will never again say 'Our gods'
to what our own hands have made . . ."
—HOSEA 14:2-3

4 "*I'm Sorry!*"

We marvel at Hosea's willingness to forgive Gomer, but sometimes asking for forgiveness can be even harder than granting it.

Imagine how difficult it would have been for Gomer to apologize to Hosea. And consider how many ways she could have gone wrong by shifting blame or being defensive. "I'm sorry that I have been committing adultery against you, husband. But you knew what I was when you married me . . ." "If you hadn't been so holier than thou . . ."

How often a poorly worded apology will lead to yet more offense and arguing! We all know what it's like to receive an apology that doesn't deliver because it's mixed with accusations or excuses: "I'm sorry that you got mad . . ." or "I'm sorry I yelled, but if you hadn't . . ."

In the passage quoted at the top of this page, Hosea actually gives the people advice on *how* to apologize to God. "Use these words," he says! "Say *this!*"

On the one hand, it may seem insincere to tell someone exactly what words to use when apologizing. But on the other hand, there are certain key elements to a good apology, all of which can

HOSEA & GOMER

be found in Hosea's advice to the Israelites. Simply put, they look like this:

Confession: "I was wrong!" (Even if you were not the only one who was wrong, own up to your part in the misunderstanding or offense, even if it seems small.)

Affirmation: "I understand why you would feel angry and hurt." (How powerful it is to be told that we've been heard and that our reaction is understood.)

Repentance: "I am going to try to not make this mistake again." (A commitment to change or to try to avoid the offense in the future reaffirms that genuine regret accompanies the apology.)

The Request: "Please forgive me!" (This isn't a demand, but a sincere appeal for forgiveness—not to be withdrawn if our mate needs more time or to talk it through further.)

How difficult it can be to take these steps. But how miraculous a well-worded and well-intentioned apology can be! As James said, "Therefore confess your sins to each other and pray for each other so that you may be healed" (James 5:16).

> *Heavenly Father,*
> *We're so good at requiring forgiveness, but so poor and lazy about giving it. Forgive us, Lord. Help us to become as serious about mastering the art of confession, apology, and forgiveness as we are about mastering the art of making love. We want to be healers and lovers and givers and forgivers to each other today! Amen.*

 Love Talk | Which part of apologizing is hardest for you? For your mate? Set aside a time when you are not angry to discuss how and where you both tend to get snagged in the process of reconciling.

196

I will show my love to the one I called "Not my loved one." I will say to those called "Not my people" "You are my people" and they will say, "You are my God."

—HOSEA 2:23

5 The Road to Redemption

Few stories in the Bible arouse our curiosity more than the story of Hosea and Gomer. We want to say to Hosea, "You forgave your wife's adultery and brought her home. But *then* what?"

Sometimes what happens *after* we grant forgiveness to our mate is as important as our original choice to forgive. Hosea had to live with the legacy of Gomer's adultery—illegitimate children, gossip in town, feelings of hurt and betrayal. And Gomer had to live with the shameful knowledge of what she'd done.

Even when we forgive our mate for a lesser offense than adultery, we often share the heartache of the consequences. A week later, when we're still paying a price somehow, it's tempting to say, "I forgive you—but look how much your mistake has cost us!"

Especially when our mate has deeply hurt us, forgiveness is usually only the first step on the road to redemption. Not only might the offended mate have to pay some price (Hosea had to pay financially as well as emotionally), but the other person must accept the lingering consequences, such as their mate's nagging distrust.

So how can we guarantee that the seed of forgiveness we grant our mate will continue to blossom into full redemption? Christ is our inspiration and our help at such times. Not only did He pay the price for our sins with His death, He committed Himself to walking *with* us through the broken glass of all our mistakes.

To go beyond forgiveness to redemption means asking, "What can we learn from this? Together, how can we cooperate with God to turn this to good?"

Sometimes as we're facing painful consequences or reminders, it helps to make a change that will symbolize the redemption we're claiming. When God relented toward Israel, He told Hosea to "show love" to Gomer. And then He changed the names He'd given Hosea's children, "I will say to those called 'Not my people,' You are my people."

For us, showing love may simply mean that we agree never to mention a certain incident again. Or it might mean something more concrete, such as eating a romantic dinner on the very same rug that we had a huge fight about buying.

Our human nature makes it so easy for us to cling to bitterness rather than pursue healing. Yet by the amazing life of Christ, we have everything we need to start over after being hurt deeply— hope, courage, humility, and understanding. And soon we discover that the price of redemption is worth the reward it brings.

> *Lord of Our Marriage,*
> *Thank You that You are able to work all things to-*
> *gether for our good, even when we've blown it (Romans*
> *8:28). Today we commit not only to forgiving one an-*
> *other, but to walking through the consequences of our*
> *mistakes together. You are our Redeemer. Your mercies*
> *are new each day. And we're confident that You will*
> *complete the good things You've started in our marriage*
> *(Philippians 1:6). We love You, Lord! Amen.*

What good things has God started in your marriage today? How could you celebrate them together?

CHAPTER ELEVEN

Esther & Xerxes

About Esther

Name: Means "a star" (Persian) "myrtle" (Jewish)
Age at Marriage: Around 15
Appearance: Extraordinarily beautiful
Personality: Loyal, prudent, confident
Family Background: Parents deceased; Esther was adopted by an older cousin, Mordecai
Place in History: Jewish queen of the Persian King Xerxes I (Ahasuerus); she saved God's people from a plot to annihilate them

About Xerxes

Name: Means "mighty man"
Age at Marriage: Unknown
Appearance: Shown in ancient art as bearded and powerfully built
Personality: Impulsive, short-sighted, but reasonable and fair
Family Background: Father was King Darius Hystaspis
Place in History: King of Persia with vast empire in 485–464 B.C.; husband to Queen Esther, who convinced him to overturn his own edict against the Jews

Wielding Power Wisely

The Book of Esther

Only two books in the Bible are named after a woman—Ruth and Esther. Ruth's is a farm story that unfolds as peacefully as breezes sighing across a grain field. By contrast, Esther's is a palace drama that descends like a firestorm in the halls of world power.

If you want great bedtime storytelling, both books are must-reads (Ruth, about 15 minutes; Esther, about 45 minutes). For centuries they have been considered among the finest examples of ancient literature. Their themes—how likable, honorable people overcome great odds in an often brutal world—are still as timely as ever.

When it comes to likable and honorable, Esther is one of the Bible's stars (in fact, her name means "star"). She's a brave and beautiful orphan with a secret that could get her killed. How could Xerxes not fall hard for her?

As her story unfolds, we see how God uses Xerxes' affection for Esther and her discretion and courage to make history. She plays the key role in delivering God's people from a plot for empire-wide genocide. Jews today read the book every year at the Festival of Purim, which still commemorates Queen Esther's role in their deliverance 2,500 years ago.

The book opens with Xerxes, king of Persia and most of the known world, getting miffed at his wife. Queen Vashti has refused to parade her charms in front of the king and his drunken friends. "If he doesn't take stern action there will be no end of discord," advisers warn the king, So the king banishes Queen Vashti as an example to other women who might be thinking of ignoring their husbands' orders.

To find a new queen for him, Xerxes' advisers suggest a beauty pageant. The king can work his way down the lineup, trying out all the most attractive girls in the kingdom. Then, they propose, "let the girl who pleases the king be queen instead of Vashti."

The king thinks the plan is terrific. (*"Where's the love story in that?"* you're wondering. *"How did this ever get in the Bible?"*)

Enter Esther. When the king's talent hunters show up at her door, she's leading a quiet life as the adopted child of her cousin, Mordecai. She has no choice but to leave with them. After 12 months of beauty treatments in the harem, Esther is taken in to the king's personal quarters. The next day, an ecstatic Xerxes announces that the contest is over. He declares Esther to be the new queen and hosts a banquet in her honor. The rest of the empire is granted a national holiday.

But Xerxes doesn't know that his lovely new queen is a Jew. A seemingly small detail at first, Esther's hidden identity soon becomes the focal point for the rest of story, sweeping her into potential peril and then, destiny . . .

What starts out as a story about a beauty contest quickly turns serious. Haman, a prideful, power-hungry official in the palace, has schemed to kill every Jew in the empire. By the time his plan falls into place, even the king seems helpless to stop it. Esther alone can intervene. But she must make her appeal to Xerxes on the grounds of love, not right or power—and in so doing she risks execution.

Sound like a made-for-Hollywood epic? Esther's story has enough plot twists to keep modern readers turning the pages. For example, the book of Esther could be described in many ways:

- *A political thriller*—about a king who, by decree, can never be wrong, but whose rash choices propel his empire from one near-disaster to another.

- *A domestic drama*—about a beautiful queen who changes history simply by inviting her husband to dinner.

- *A historical account*—of how plans for a genocide are turned into a national celebration of deliverance.

- *A morality play*—about the collision between good and evil, believer and unbeliever, a vulnerable girl and her husband's brutal, scheming adviser.

- *A character study*—of one Person (God) who is never mentioned, not even once.

And in God's own surprising way, Esther's story can show us some wonderful truths about marriage. If we can get past the cultural differences, we find two people who treat each other with love and respect even when they're surrounded by users and traitors. The royal couple survive a crisis in both their marriage and their kingdom by making sure the enemy stays outside their marriage.

So, add one more description to the list. The book of Esther is finally: *a love story.*

Not surprisingly, you'll find that power is a recurring theme here—the power of a woman over a man, the power of a man over a woman, and the power of God to rule events from behind the scenes. Xerxes and Esther can teach us by example how influence and advantage in our relationships can be used wisely, with respect for the other person and for mutual good.

Then the king's personal attendants pro-
posed, "Let a search be made for beautiful
young virgins for the king. Let the king appoint
commissioners in every province of his realm
to bring all these beautiful girls into the harem
at the citadel of Susa. . . .Then let the girl who
pleases the king be queen instead of Vashti."
This advice appealed to the king, and he
followed it.

—ESTHER 2:2-4

1 *Power and Love*

At first glance, the story of Esther and Xerxes assaults our
modern sensibilities. A king who banishes his queen when she refuses to be ogled by his friends? And who then collects a harem of
beautiful virgins for his personal pleasure?

But Xerxes' behavior was standard for the times. As king of the
world's dominant empire, he wielded unlimited power and was
viewed as a god.

Both Persian and Jewish law of the period considered a woman
more as property than as a person. Each morning, Jewish men
prayed, "I thank God that He did not make me a Gentile, or a
slave, or a woman."

Doesn't sound too promising for an orphaned Jewish girl
entering into marriage, does it? Interestingly, it is Xerxes' incredible
power advantage that sets us up for a surprise in this story.
We expect a master-slave relationship (or worse), but instead find
evidence of mutual respect, trust, and support.

He wasn't exactly Mr. Sensitive, but King Xerxes—even when
he held all the cards—treated his wife in ways we ordinary mortals
could emulate:

- *He responded to her vulnerability with protection.*
  By extending the scepter when she approached him
  to make her request, Xerxes covered her with his
  acceptance and authority, thus sparing her life
  (Esther 5:2).

- *He wanted to please her.* Repeatedly, Xerxes asks
  Esther, "What is your request? It will be given you"
  (5:3,6; 7:2).

- *He shared his power.* First Xerxes offers to share his
  kingdom with Esther (5:3,6; 7:2). Later he shares his
  authority: "So Queen Esther . . . wrote with full authority to confirm this second letter concerning
  Purim" (9:29).

- *He took his wife's advice.* Xerxes repeatedly asks for the
  advice of his court officials. But he also takes Esther's
  suggestions, including the one to overrule Haman's
  decree (7:3; 8:5; 9:13).

- *He was willing to be wrong.* Xerxes must have known
  he'd made a big mistake in letting Haman misuse his
  position. But he was humble enough to seek his wife's
  help to make things right (8:8).

For centuries, male dominance has brought disharmony and
injury into marriages. Christian men have sometimes misapplied
Scripture and twisted history to excuse selfish attitudes and brutal
behavior toward their wives. Esther's story stands strongly against
these wrongs.

Today, husbands and wives both hold scepters of influence in
their hands. Some times one partner holds the power, while the
other is left holding only vulnerability and need. At other times,
our positions are reversed.

In your own marriage today remember that every opportunity
to dominate is also an invitation to use power for good—to serve,
to build up, to make the one you love glad just to be alive.

O God,

You are the King of kings, yet when I was lost and defeated by sin, You gave away Your power for me. You chose to die for me so I could live. Help me show that kind of power and love in my marriage today. Amen.

Love Talk

In what areas or ways do each of you hold the upper hand in your marriage—and how willing are you to share that power today?

"If it pleases the king," she said, "and if he regards me with favor and thinks it the right thing to do, and if he is pleased with me, let an order be written overruling the dispatches that Haman . . . wrote to destroy the Jews in all the king's province."

—ESTHER 8:5

2 *A Beauty and a Beast*

A beautiful woman, a powerful man, and a political landscape of intrigue, betrayal, and dangerous secrets . . .

If you didn't know better, you'd think we were talking about Samson and Delilah. In fact, Esther and Delilah have much in common. Both women were pursued by men of legendary power. And both set out to get something they wanted from those men. Yet one woman was a beauty; the other, a beast.

What sets them apart is how each used her persuasive powers, and toward what end. Although Esther helped King Xerxes become a better king, Delilah caused Samson to betray himself and his calling. And though Esther risked her own life in approaching King Xerxes, Delilah risked Samson's for her own selfish purposes.

Swaying our spouse in one direction or another is a real part of married life. But there's a right way and a wrong way. Next time you approach your mate with an agenda, keep Esther's example in mind:

- *Check to see if your request and motives line up with God's.* What Esther wanted—to save her people—was God's clear will. And she took time to fast and pray before she approached Xerxes.

- *Ask whether what you want is good for both of you.* Esther's request was good for both her and her husband. Xerxes needed to know the truth about Haman's conspiracy.

- *Choose the right time and place.* Esther invited Xerxes to a banquet partly for the purpose of trapping Haman. By doing so, she chose an opportune time—while he was enjoying her company and her meal—to make her request.

- *Be straightforward, not manipulative.* When Esther finally informed Xerxes of her problem, she put it to him plainly. And then she let him know exactly what she hoped for in the way of response.

- *Affirm your confidence in your mate's wisdom.* Esther's careful choice of words helped Xerxes feel respected, rather than challenged. "If the king thinks . . . If it pleases the king . . ."

We all know what it's like to want something from our mates, and to want it very badly. If we check our hearts as well as our words, we can approach our spouse with grace and confidence.

When Paul wrote his first letter to Timothy, he made a difficult request—"command certain men not to teach" (1 Timothy 1:3). Paul knew how stressful this advice would be for the young, kind pastor to carry out, so he followed up with reassurance: "The goal of this command is love, which comes from a pure heart and a good conscience and a sincere faith" (1:5).

If the goal of our request is love, we can turn our most challenging confrontations into something beautiful for us and for our marriage.

> *Lord,*
> *Help me to approach my mate with my requests honestly and with loving consideration. Help me to only ask for what is in keeping with Your will and in keeping with our love. Amen.*

How can you try to change a spouse's mind while keeping his or her dignity intact? What are the traps to avoid? Ask your mate for ideas.

Go, gather together all the Jews who are in Susa, and fast for me. Do not eat or drink for three days, night or day. I and my maids will fast as you do. When this is done, I will go to the king, even though it is against the law. And if I perish, I perish.

—ESTHER 4:15-16

3 *Source of Power*

What happened? In chapter two, Esther was the toast of the empire, the talk of every girl dreaming of a prince charming. Now she's fasting, preparing herself for possible execution.

And her danger is very real. The Greek historian Herodotus reported that to even lay eyes on the face of a Persian king was a privilege granted only to his family and to seven of his closest advisers (mentioned in Esther 1:14). This extreme measure was meant to protect the king from assassination and to show him honor. (Jews had a unique perspective on this custom—Moses taught that no one could see God and live.)

Picture the scene for a moment: Esther pauses outside the king's throne room. She is about to discover not only her fate, but that of her people. Will the king be outraged at her presumption? Will he forgive her for keeping her Jewish identity a secret? Will his affection for her be deep enough to compel him to reach for the scepter?

As she enters the inner court, gasps of alarm ripple around the room. Xerxes looks up. Esther's heart catches. Then she sees the look in his eyes—it is gladness—and she watches with relief as he stretches the gold scepter in her direction. . . .

So where did Esther get such courage?

Recall that when she first heard Mordecai's plea for help she didn't boast, "I'm blessed with the empire's best looks and charm. And I have that man around my little finger. I know I can take care of the problem."

Instead, Esther understood that whenever something that belongs to God is threatened—whether a nation or a marriage—any victory will have to be a spiritual victory. She knew that the real power to save herself or alter the course of events didn't lay in her husband's hands at all, but in God's.

The feasts she prepared for Xerxes said to him: "I have good things and I want to share them with you. You are important to me."

But first, she fasted, saying to her King of kings, "I am weak. I have nothing, and I'm depending on You for everything. You are my Lord."

When problems come, how easy it is to rush in with our own solutions, or imagine that our mate is the only one who can fix things. But Esther reminds us that when crises come, the best place to begin is on our knees before God. No personal strengths or abilities today can take the place of a husband's or wife's prayers. Prayer is the humbling that comes before our courage and God's surprising answers.

> *Dear Lord of This Marriage,*
>   *You are the source of power for our relationship. You are our protector, our deliverer, and our friend. Your blessing is our greatest wealth (Proverbs 10:22, TLB). We bow before You and praise You. By Your power, overcome all that threatens Your purposes in our lives today. Amen.*

Love Talk Is there some daunting challenge or desire in your marriage that is important enough to you to fast and pray about it? How could you help each other to take this step?

Before a girl's turn came to go in to King Xerxes, she had to complete twelve months of beauty treatments prescribed for the women, six months with oil of myrrh and six with perfumes and cosmetics.

—ESTHER 2:12

4 The Power of Beauty

Our culture is preoccupied with beauty. Just read the titles to the magazine articles: *"Five Minutes a Day to Thin Thighs," "Fall Fashions to Make His Jaw Drop," "Perfect Hair Every Day."* And is there any magazine Cindy Crawford hasn't graced the cover of?

Esther's story reminds us that mankind has always put great emphasis on physical attractiveness. In fact, Revlon would have done well in Persia. Though Esther "was lovely in form and features" (Esther 2:7), she spent an entire year getting beauty treatments. Scholars tell us that Esther would have been lavished with massages, scents, oils, hair curling, rouge for her lips and cheeks, and paint for her eyes (cf. 2:12).

The Bible makes it clear that God created physical beauty and intended for us to enjoy it. We can see it in Adam's delight over Eve and in the gushing tributes to beauty in the Song of Songs.

Yet the Bible is equally clear that physical charms aren't as important as spiritual or "inner" beauty. "Beauty is fleeting," Solomon wrote, "but a woman who fears the Lord is to be praised" (Proverbs 31:30). Peter counseled wives, "Your beauty should not come from outward adornment, . . . Instead, it should be that of your inner self, the unfading beauty of a gentle and quiet spirit, which is of great worth in God's sight" (1 Peter 3:3-4).

Esther must have possessed a stunning combination of beauty, inside and out. Even in a harem of such splendor, something about Esther won over everyone, including the harem master.

And surely Xerxes was looking for more than a pretty face. To do his reputation justice and to fulfill her role as queen, his new partner would need to command attention with her bearing, her words, and her personality, as well as with her looks. We're told that Esther fit this double-bill: "The king was attracted to Esther more than to any other women, and she won his favor and approval more than any of the other virgins" (2:17).

This doesn't mean we should care nothing about our looks, or that we shouldn't love to hear our spouse say, "You look smashing." But it does mean that we need the assurance that our partner's love for us isn't dependent on our looks or the size of our girth. Unlike physical beauty, spiritual beauty is something we can nurture in ourselves and our mate as long as we live.

Mike Mason writes, "Is a wife . . . losing her curves, her good looks? Then her husband must renounce his attachment to those things, at just as deep a level as the wife herself must do. Rather than lament the loss of her youth, both must learn to rejoice in the new and more lasting thing that comes into being."

As married lovers, we get to enjoy each other's physical bodies over many years of life together. But we also have the power to see deeply into our mate's soul—deeper than anyone else—and to prize and celebrate the beauty we find there. We know that Xerxes appreciated Esther. Yet she understood and appreciated him too, or she could never have won his ardor and loyalty.

Attractiveness is a powerful gift in marriage—but it doesn't compare to the power we have when we appreciate and affirm to the world the total appeal of our other half.

Heavenly Father,

Thank You for making beautiful bodies and beautiful persons. Help me see and value my spouse today like You do. Amen.

 Try to see your spouse as if for the first time. What appealing qualities do you notice? How could you make him or her feel compellingly beautiful today?

> Do not think that because you are in the king's
> house you alone of all the Jews will escape. For if
> you remain silent at this time, relief and deliver-
> ance for the Jews will arise from another place,
> but you and your father's family will perish. And
> who knows but that you have come to royal posi-
> tion for such a time as this?
>
> —Mordecai (ESTHER 4:13-14)

The Power of
5 Impossible Situations

Writers sometimes say that to make a story all you have to do is create an interesting character and get him in trouble. A *great* story happens, they say, when the reader *becomes* the character—and the trouble seems insurmountable.

Imagine Queen Esther for a moment . . .

She is standing by a window in her private quarters. Caged songbirds twitter behind her. Marble tables set with flowers and fruit wait for her pleasure. But the queen gazes out into the court-yard. In her hand, she holds a scribbled note. The maids notice that it is trembling. Something has happened, terrible news. When she turns back into the room, Esther seems somehow less like a queen and more like a child far, far from home.

She looks at her attendants and says simply, "I must prepare to die."

This scene from chapter four brings together the orphan-girl-turned-queen that we've come to care about, and the insurmountable trouble caused by the king's death warrant against the Jews. With her cousin's challenge—"Perhaps you have come to your position for just such a time as this"—ringing in her ears, Esther makes her decision. She sends a message back to him: "I will go to the king, even though it is against the law. And if I perish, I perish" (Esther 4:16).

Think of the marriage circumstances Esther encountered that seemed all wrong, if not impossible to deal with. Perhaps you're in one:

- You're married to an unbeliever who makes choices that go against your values and preferences.

- You're married to an unpredictable, potentially dangerous person.

- You feel cut off from family or other supportive relationships.

- Your true identity—the things about you that mean the most to you personally—remains unknown to your spouse, and you suspect if he or she knew, trouble or rejection would follow.

- For much too long, you've not even been sure that your marriage partner loves you or is committed to the relationship you share.

Esther experienced all these troubles, only to discover there was no way out except to walk forward—straight ahead into what she feared. And it was at that moment she became the heroine we admire.

Where is the power in impossible circumstances? God told Paul, "My power is made perfect in weakness" (2 Corinthians 12:9). Esther might add, "Only then can God show His hidden presence and bring glory to Himself."

God allows every marriage to sometimes experience desperate needs and impossible circumstances. It is all for a reason. When we come to the end of ourselves, God steps in to act. And it is then that we discover that we too were born for such a time, and such a marriage, as this.

Lord,

Help me to release to You the things in my life which seem insurmountable. Your ways are beyond my ways. I can't understand or predict how You will work. But I know You will. Help me to be faithful and brave. Help me to see that my troubles are opportunities for Your saving grace to be revealed. Amen.

What seemingly impossible situation in the past has been an opening for God, who "in all things . . . works for the good of those who love him" (Romans 8:28)? Ask Him to do the same for something you face together today.

CHAPTER TWELVE

Joseph & Mary

About Joseph

Name: Means "increaser"

Age at Marriage: Often assumed to be mid-thirties or older

Appearance: Unknown

Personality: Faithful, reliable, described as "righteous"

Family Background: Son of Jacob, a descendant of King David; his hometown was Bethlehem; he was a carpenter by trade

Place in History: The loyal husband of Mary, mother of Jesus

About Mary

Name: Means "strong"

Age at Marriage: Unknown, probably about 15

Appearance: Unknown

Personality: Gracious, full of faith, forthright, willing, wise

Family Background: From Nazareth in Galilee; like Joseph, she was from the tribe of Judah

Place in History: The virgin who became the mother of Jesus, Son of God

Discovering Your Destiny

Luke 1–2; Matthew 1

It's a story most of us have heard since we were tots in zippered sleepers, curled up on our mother's lap: *"One starry night, long, long ago, an angel came to visit a girl named Mary . . ."*

We've seen it acted out by children wearing bathrobes and cotton-ball beards: *"Mary, the innkeeper said that since you're expecting a baby, we can stay in his barn . . ."* (A cow moos off-stage.)

We've heard it caroled from frosty doorsteps: *"Away in a manger, no place for a bed, the little Lord Jesus lay down His sweet head. . . ."*

And preached from pulpits: *"For God so loved the world, that he gave his one and only Son . . ."*

The Christmas Story is probably the planet's best-known baby story. But now that we're out of zippered sleepers, we might dare to look at the familiar account from a fresh perspective—as a marriage story.

Let's start by taking a closer look at the main characters:

The fiancé, Joseph, was a carpenter from the tribe of Judah who could trace his lineage back to King David. When he asked for young Mary's hand in marriage, he had home-building and furniture in mind, not Caesar's tax plans or Old Testament prophecies. But his response to the angel Gabriel's instructions proves him to have been an even-tempered, reliable, and deeply pious man—a good marriage prospect in any small town.

The betrothed, Mary, was of marriageable age—probably about 15. A virgin, she was concerned for Joseph's reputation. And like her husband-to-be, she was a person of sincere spiritual commitments. Moments before she discovered that she would become the mother of the Savior, Mary probably lay on her bed thinking about the life which lay ahead with the carpenter, not about the Messiah. But her response to the angel, "May it be to me as you have said," and her actions in the months that followed, show her to be clear-headed, brave, and steadfast.

You could say that Mary and Joseph had all the makings of a "perfect couple." Yet God asked them to travel a very difficult road together. We all know the facts and chronology of their story—from their engagement, through the pregnancy and birth, to the flight to Egypt and the resettlement in Nazareth where Jesus grew up. Think about all the stresses to their relationship this very human couple encountered during their engagement:

- An unexpected premarital pregnancy.

- Angelic interventions.

- The knowledge (before they'd lived together even for a day) that their marriage and parenting skills would be required to raise God's Son.

- Life-changing choices.

- Extreme changes of plans.

And then after marriage:

- A wedding clouded by rumors.

- Rigorous travel during the final weeks of pregnancy.

- Their first child born in a barn (parents just passing through).

- The knowledge that their baby was on the king's "Most Wanted for Execution" list.

- Emergency relocation to Egypt (nursing infant in arms).

- Exiled in a foreign land, separated from all relatives and support groups.

And only a year had passed since Joseph's proposal of marriage!

When you think about it, God could have avoided all these complications. He could have brought Jesus into the world any way He pleased. He could have chosen a couple with a proven marriage—or skipped the marriage (and parents) altogether. Instead, the God of the universe chose an ordinary couple with only the promise of love—as if to say, *"Married love, even at its most vulnerable, is exactly the place I want to begin my redemption story."*

Our own marriage stories also begin with only the promise of love. Everything is potential, nothing's guaranteed, and we can expect trouble ahead. Yes, God chose Mary and Joseph's marriage for a unique destiny. But if we look more closely at this couple, we also see our own marriage: a man and a woman traveling together step by step into God's amazing plan.

We can draw help and inspiration from Mary and Joseph's radical choice to love, obey, and trust. Like them, our faith in God and each other will surely be severely tested—if it hasn't already been. We'll experience surprising complications and often have more questions than answers. But like Mary and Joseph, we too can let life's twists and turns bring us together to kneel before the Savior, and share Him gladly with others who seek Him.

This is how the birth of Jesus Christ came about: His mother Mary was pledged to be married to Joseph, but before they came together, she was found to be with child through the Holy Spirit. Because Joseph her husband was a righteous man and did not want to expose her to public disgrace, he had in mind to divorce her quietly.
—MATTHEW 1:18-19

1 A Witness to the World

Scripture doesn't tell us anything about that painful period of time between when Joseph heard the news that Mary was pregnant and when the angel appeared to him in a dream to explain. But we can imagine Joseph's anguished thoughts—*How could my bride-to-be have done such a thing!?*

And what about the wedding feast? We don't know if it was well attended, if the bride looked happy beneath her veil, or if rumors and gossip dampened the festivities. What we do know is that the marriage that would play a big part in the deliverance of the world from shame, began under the threat of disgrace.

In many ways, what God asked Mary and Joseph to do is the same as He asks of every married believer: *to bring Jesus—through our words, our life, and our love—into the world.* And He really doesn't want us to wait until we have everything together—tidy, safe, and spotless—to do so.

Sometimes it's easy to forget that it is not just our wedding ceremonies that take place in public and make a statement to the world. So do our marriages. It's good to ask, what is our marriage saying today? Are we bringing the good news of redemption, too?

Every marriage can be a love story from God to the world—in very practical ways:

- In how we treat each other, privately and in public (Matthew 1:19-25).

- In how we raise our children, seeing them as gifts from God, not just for us but for our world (Luke 2:39-40).

- By creating the kind of problem-solving, hope-giving homes that attract and influence others (Luke 2:16-20).

- By being husbands and wives who are quick to give God the credit for our blessings (Luke 2:46-50).

This isn't just more "try harder" advice for already overloaded husbands and wives. God wants to touch our world today through who we are—with our difficult personalities, less-than-perfect marriages, disappointments, and "impossible" circumstances. As we choose to forgive, to love, to bravely believe, we can join in Mary and Joseph's amazing destiny—sharing the Good News of Jesus with the world.

Joseph could have balked, you know. After all, things were not turning out at all well—especially in the eyes of religious folk. Instead, "he did what the the angel of the Lord had commanded him" (Matthew 1:24). And in so doing, this very ordinary man in a pickle allowed God's light to burst out over a dark and needy world.

If we'll look up from our circumstances to what God is inviting us to share in, we can do the same.

Heavenly Father,

My marriage partner and I want to be a witness to the world of Your saving love. Your love has reached down to us and changed us. Thank You, Father. Thank You for Your blessings. Use us just as we are to bless others for Your glory. Amen.

What one gift of love could you find the courage to share with another person or family today?

When Joseph woke up, he did what the angel of the Lord commanded him and took Mary home as his wife. But he had no union with her until she gave birth to a son.
—MATTHEW 1:24-25

2 Joseph's Miracle

Martin Luther once said that there were three miracles of Christmas: the first was that God became a man; the second was that Mary conceived; and the third was that Mary believed. And this last miracle, Luther said, was the greatest of all.

Why? Perhaps because Mary's miracle was the only one that required something human—belief. And yet it was necessary in order to make everything else possible.

But there's a fourth miracle that Luther doesn't mention—the miracle that *Joseph* believed. Think about this for a moment. Mary at least had intimate knowledge of her own body and could be certain that she was both pregnant *and a virgin.* Joseph had no such physical evidence.

Remember, Joseph wasn't a theologian; he was a working man with calluses and cracked fingernails. He couldn't have understood all the nuances of his dream or exactly what the words—"You are to give him the name Jesus, because he will save his people from their sins"—could mean.

In Matthew, we're told something else startling about Joseph: "But he had no union with her until she gave birth to a son." Night after night, he held back his sexual desire for his new bride.

Clearly, Joseph's faith had to reach further than just making the right response at the right moment. Both he and Mary had to choose faith again and again. When Mary became the target of gossip. When Joseph's friends talked behind his back.

When we first hear God whisper an invitation into our hearts—even if it sounds difficult or outrageous—we may answer, "Yes, I will do that. I believe You." His invitation to us might be something like "Don't bring that sore point up with your husband again," or "It's time to let go of that selfish use of your time and money," or "I want you to serve Me."

But our "yes" is only the first step. Any destiny good enough for God to give us, especially for our marriages, will require us not only to *receive* it in faith, but to *continue* in faith—long after the excitement of our courtship fades and we discover that our partner is forgetful, careless, and clueless.

In fact, it is usually at the worst possible moments in our marriages—when nothing seems to be going according to plan and everything we believe about our mate is up for grabs—that we're asked to choose faith, and our marriage, all over again.

The writer of Hebrews describes faith as "being sure of what we hope for and certain of what we do not see" (Hebrews 11:1). He could have called it "the fourth miracle of Christmas"—just ask Joseph.

> *Heavenly Father,*
> *Today I want to experience the fourth miracle of Christmas. Help me to believe in my mate and in Your plan for our lives, even when it all seems impossible and when everything about who and where we are appears to be at odds with the plan You've whispered in our ear because You have something extraordinary in mind! Amen.*

What aspects of your marriage continue to require a leap of faith in each other and in God?

*The angel said to her, "Do not be afraid,
Mary . . ."*

—LUKE 1: 26; 31-32

*An angel of the Lord appeared to him in a
dream and said, "Joseph son of David, do not be
afraid . . ."*

—MATTHEW 1:20-21

3 *Africa or Detroit?*

Imagine how differently things might have turned out if God had let only one partner in on the big news. Instead, God sent an angel to speak to *both* Mary and Joseph about what was to come. How comforting it must have been for each to learn an angel had also visited the other.

In fact, the messages they received were very similar. God said, "Do not be afraid." He announced the pregnancy and told them both what to name the baby (ruling out arguments over Zerubbabel versus Amminadab). Then He explained the significance of Jesus' birth.

God wanted Joseph and Mary to be united in their knowledge of His will for them. And this is still true for us today. We can be confident that when God wants to do something big in our marriage, He's going to talk with *both* of us about it sooner or later. In fact, being in agreement with our spouse is one way we know that we're hearing God clearly.

This isn't to say that God won't ever speak His will to only one of us. But why would God leave us hanging with only an argument about what He wants instead of agreement? A one-flesh marriage was His idea in the first place.

So what happens when you and your mate sense a different direction from God? When one of you says, "I think God's calling us to be missionaries in Africa," and the other says, "I think He wants us to move to Detroit to be closer to my mother"?

There's probably some truth in what both of you hear. Ask yourselves: What does common sense say? What do circumstances point toward? What about the advice of those we trust? Could the differences be a matter of timing or sequence? Have we checked out our motives and priorities? What does Scripture teach? Then wait quietly until you're both sure. It's never God's idea to drive a wedge into a marriage that honors Him.

And you can count on the fact that God is never trying to hide your destiny from you. The advice of this Scripture always holds true, "In all your ways, acknowledge him and he will make your paths straight" (Proverbs 3:6).

> *Heavenly Father,*
> *You are not a God of confusion. Your wisdom is available to us if we ask, and today we ask You to make Your way known to us, individually and together. Open our eyes. Unplug our ears. We don't want to miss Your best. And during our times of uncertainty, help us remember that searching and waiting can be a necessary part of Your plan, too. Amen.*

 Love Talk

What messages from God to each of you, and to your marriage, have you heard many times? What have you heard most recently? Talk about these leadings today, write them down, and remind each other of them often.

While they were there, the time came for the baby to be born, and she gave birth to her firstborn, a son. She wrapped him in cloths and placed him in a manger, because there was no room for them in the inn.

—LUKE 2:6

A Dressed-Down Performance

4

Many of us have fond childhood memories of acting out The Christmas Story. Maybe you were a pillow-stuffed sheep or an angel with foil wings. You probably remember the spotlights, the music, and the applause.

Of course, the original scene was much different: cold, damp, and smelly. As performances go, it was a disaster; and as birthing rooms go, no place to have a baby.

Joseph must have despaired. Here was his new wife about to give birth to the Savior, and he couldn't even provide her with a bed. Was this really God's plan? Or had he imagined the whole thing?

One of the greatest challenges God gives us in marriage is to be able to determine His will for us. Sometimes, just when we think we're in the center of His plans, things go terribly wrong. You and your spouse both felt led to a certain church, but now it's in upheaval. The house you bought by faith turns out to need major repairs. Or "the door God opened" for your husband to go to graduate school suddenly slams shut.

We see from Joseph and Mary's story that things can appear to be going poorly—like Joseph's timing in Bethlehem—when in fact

God's plan is right on track. So, how do we know if we're in a difficult spot because we're supposed to be or because we made a wrong turn? The Christmas Story suggests:

Look for shepherds. God usually sends encouragement in the form of other people to let us know that we're in His will. Imagine Joseph's relief and joy on delivery night when shepherds suddenly rushed into the smelly stable and announced, "Hey, angels appeared to us and told us about your baby, Jesus!"

Prepare your camels. Sometimes God changes plans midstream. God sent Joseph and Mary from Nazareth to Bethlehem, then on to Egypt. Only many months later did their little family get back home. The path of God's will is not always straight and obvious. Nor is it unchanging. Ask God together, "Is this *still* the direction?"

Get past the smelly stables. God's idea of success is different from ours. He wants to be glorified through our weaknesses. And some of His greatest opportunities to reveal His grace, mercy, and love come when we have no resources of our own. A deeper look at Mary and Joseph's manger fiasco reveals God's desire to come to man with the humblest of means for the grandest of purposes.

God's will for our marriage rarely appears to be a perfect performance, and we're not always well-rehearsed for our parts. But the One who is directing our marriage delights in every fumbling step we take to honor Him.

> *Heavenly Father,*
> *You are the Lord of palaces and stables, the Leader of wise men and shepherds, the King of angels and village girls. Come into our home today. Come into our marriages, and our hearts. Bring Your gracious presence. We will worship You, Oh Father. We surrender our expectations of grand performances, and prepare instead for Your purposes, however surprising they might be. Because You are worthy, and we love You. Amen.*

Most couples regularly review the checkbook and social calendar together. Today take time for a "destiny inventory." Ask, "What is God calling us to do and become as a couple—and how are we doing at fulfilling that?"

*So Joseph also went up from the town of
Nazareth in Galilee to Judea, to Bethlehem the
town of David, because he belonged to the house
and line of David. . . . While they were there . . .
she gave birth to her firstborn, a son. She
wrapped him in cloths and placed him in a
manger, because there was no room for them in
the inn.*

—LUKE 2:4-7

5 Destination: Home

When Mary went into labor with baby Jesus, she and Joseph
were far from home and, for all practical purposes, homeless. Yet
we sense God's satisfaction with the course of events in Luke's
simple statement: "This is how the birth of Jesus came about." No
apologies, thank you.

Because Joseph was a carpenter, we can probably assume he
built Mary a home when they finally settled in Nazareth. But in the
meantime, his love for her must have felt like her only earthly
shelter.

In ancient Israel, one who committed a capital crime could flee
to a city of refuge and claim sanctuary from execution. Joseph was
Mary's refuge:

- He shielded her from possible death by stoning—the
  punishment for suspected adultery.

- He protected her from gossip and social rejection by
  marrying her.

- He saved her from insecurity. The shepherds and
  magi didn't find a single parent worrying about the
  future, but a family (Luke 2:16).

Apparently, Jesus never forgot the humble conditions of His birth. Although a carpenter like His earthly father, He spent most of His adult life with "no place to lay his head" (Matthew 8:20). And we hear an echo of this in His assurance to His disciples, "In my Father's house are many rooms" (John 14:2)—rooms for the pregnant, weary, and homeless; rooms for anyone in need of God's sheltering love.

Today our houses provide us with endless opportunities to spend time, money, and energy. We can get so distracted caring for, cleaning, or decorating our houses that we neglect the real work of creating a home for our families. We're used to thinking of home-making as something we do for kids, but let's not forget that it is one of the fundamental comforts a husband and wife give each other.

- We provide emotional, physical, and spiritual safety.

- We promise unconditional love and acceptance.

- We say in a hundred ways, "We belong together, here!"

- We provide for, and are sensitive to, each other's needs.

- We're loyal to each other—against all rumor and criticism; in the face of failure; in spite of disappointments (our motto is "I believe in you, babe!").

God doesn't want to take away our houses. But He does want us to hold loosely all the props of home—our comfort, furniture, two-car garages, and our endlessly-in-need-of-mowing lawns—so we can *truly* find home—safety, acceptance, protection, belonging, and love—like Joseph and Mary did in one another's arms.

Heavenly Father,

Thank You that my spouse and I can experience home in a loving relationship. Help us to give the gift of home to each other as well as to our children, realizing that home is not about amassing things, but about surrounding love. Thank You, Jesus, that You experienced homelessness so that we can know the comfort and peace of home, now and eternally. Amen.

List 3 to 5 aspects of living together that capsulize "home" (making a sanctuary) for each other. These could be as simple as kissing each other at the door or baking an apple pie, or as far-reaching as staying out of debt. Don't let a day go by without making home special for the one you love.

Study Guides

1. *Adam & Eve*
Discovering the Meaning of Marriage

Marriage Puzzlers

Real life questions for today:

- Sometimes my partner makes a mistake that jeopardizes both of us. Isn't blame—assigning fault—appropriate and necessary? Or because we are one in God's eyes, are we both responsible for errors we make as a couple?

- When does a couple's "oneness" become a problem? What is the difference between healthy unity and unhealthy entanglement? How can we maintain our separateness as people even as we try to be one?

- Is it better to be married to someone we feel a lot in common with, or to a spouse who completes us because they're so different from us? How can a couple make the most of their differences?

- Should a husband always assume the ultimate responsibility for providing food and shelter for his family? Is this what God meant by His decrees following the Fall?

- We are told to "leave" mother and father, but also to honor them. If a spouse and an in-law don't get along, when should loyalty to the spouse take preference?

Tell Yourself the Truth—"One Flesh or One Mess?"

A self-quiz for couples.

1. If my spouse truly knew everything about me—my deepest, ugliest sins—it would change his or her love for me.

a. agree   b. somewhat agree   c. somewhat disagree   d. disagree

237

2. I accept and respect the unique qualities of the opposite sex.
a. disagree   b. somewhat disagree   c. somewhat agree   d. agree

3. In our marriage, our gender differences still bring more trouble than help.
a. yes   b. generally yes   c. generally no   d. no

4. We have arrived at a clear picture of each other's strengths (they're amazing and encouraging) and weaknesses (they're disgusting and burdensome)—and our love is still growing.
a. no, not yet   b. generally no   c. generally yes   d. yes

5. My mate and I agree on the big issues of moral standards and spiritual decisions.
a. rarely or never   b. sometimes   c. often   d. nearly always or always

6. My mate's desires or words can sway me to act against my conscience.
a. rarely or never   b. sometimes   c. often   d. nearly always or always

7. My mate and I work together well to accomplish stressful or difficult tasks.
a. rarely or never   b. sometimes   c. often   d. nearly always or always

8. We are able to accept responsibility for our own actions, and try to support each other, even when dumb mistakes are made (we've thrown out the Blame Game).
a. rarely or never   b. sometimes   c. often   d. nearly always or always

How did you score on accepting your gender differences and reaching for unity?

a's = 1 point
b's = 2 points
c's = 3 points
d's = 4 points

If you scored 8–15, you struggle a lot with gender issues and building unity.

If you scored 16–25, understanding and respecting your differences is important to you, but you know you still have quite a ways to go.

If you scored 26–32, you care deeply about unity despite differences, and you're mostly successful at building a "one-flesh" life together.

What Else Does the Bible Say?

Read and consider other related Scriptures.

Male and female: Song of Songs 4:1-5; 5:9-16

Marriage: Proverbs 5:18-20; 12:4; Mark 12:18-25; 1 Corinthians 7:1-16

Sexuality and passion: Leviticus 18:6-23; Proverbs 5; Song of Songs 5:4

Blame and responsibility: Deuteronomy 24:16; Psalm 51; Jeremiah 31:30

Shame and forgiveness: Psalm 51; Luke 17:3; Romans 8:1-17; and 10:11

Life after the Fall: Psalm 138:7; Isaiah 43:1-5; Nahum 1:7; Matthew 13:1-30

2. The Patriarchs & Their Wives
Moving Forward in Faith

Marriage Puzzlers

Real life questions for today:

- Do you think that it is good for a marriage when one partner tends to have faith, and the other spouse plays the role of "skeptic"? How might this work well? How or when might it become a problem?

- How does a couple determine whether they need more faith for a promise God gave them, or whether they might have heard wrong?

- Is it possible to still have faith and yet act (as Abraham did with Hagar) on a back-up plan? How do you think God views this kind of caution—with understanding, with disappointment, with rejection?

- Is there something wrong if a couple doesn't sense any significant personal promises from God for their life?

- How does the simple act of living by faith and waiting in hope change how we treat each other or how we handle challenges?

Tell Yourself the Truth—"Keeping Faith"

A self-quiz for couples.

1. My spouse and I have a history of living by faith even when circumstances would argue against what we are committed to achieving or becoming.
a. disagree   b. somewhat disagree   c. somewhat agree   d. agree

2. I can talk freely to my spouse about my doubts and concerns without fear that his or her own faith will crumble because I'm feeling afraid.
a. disagree   b. somewhat disagree   c. somewhat agree   d. agree

3. I look for ways to encourage and build up my spouse's faith in his or her most cherished (and perhaps impossible) dreams and endeavors:
a. never   b. rarely   c. occasionally   d. frequently

4. My spouse or I have a hard time believing in some of the most basic promises in God's Word, such as provision for our daily needs or assurance of His unfailing love.

a. agree   b. somewhat agree   c. somewhat disagree   d. disagree

5. I allow my emotions, rather than what I believe, to determine my level of confidence in God for me or my marriage.

a. almost always   b. often   c. occasionally   d. rarely

6. Like Moses, my first reaction to a radical call or promise from God is to argue about its feasibility or to doubt that God is talking to the right person.

a. frequently   b. occasionally   c. rarely   d. never

7. My spouse and I keep track of what we're praying for by faith and how God answers us so that we can be encouraged and thankful.

a. rarely or never   b. occasionally   c. often   d. always

8. I do my part to partner with God in what I'm seeking, combining wisdom, perseverance, and common sense with my faith.

a. never   b. rarely   c. occasionally   d. frequently

How did you score?

a's = 1 point
b's = 2 points
c's = 3 points
d's = 4 points

If you scored 8–15, you and your mate struggle with rising above circumstances and living by faith in God. What could you do to make some breakthroughs in this area?

If you scored 16–25, living by faith is a real and growing experience for you and your spouse, but not as often as you'd like. Based on your answers, in what areas do you see opportunities for change?

If you scored 26–32, you and your mate experience a lot of the blessings and benefits (and real spiritual stresses) of living by faith.

What Else Does the Bible Say?

Read and consider other related Scriptures.

Bridging our differences: Romans 14:17-19; 15:5-7; 1 Corinthians 1:10; 12:12-31

Inner beauty: Romans 12:12; 2 Corinthians 2:15; Galatians 5:22; Philippians 4:8

Strength for the journey: Isaiah 41:10; Romans 8:38-39; Philippians 4:13

Faith: Isaiah 40:31; Matthew 17:20; Hebrews 11:1,6; 1 Peter 1:7-9; 1 John 5:4

God's promises: Deuteronomy 33:27; Ezekiel 12:25; Matthew 24:35; 2 Peter 1:4

3. Isaac & Rebekah
Finding the Right One

Marriage Puzzlers

Real life questions for today:

- What if our parents don't approve of our prospective mates, or we as parents disapprove of our child's choice for a mate? How far should parents go to discourage what they believe will be a bad marriage? And what about after the marriage has taken place?

- If God's not involved in the decision-making of a marriage partner, can we still expect Him to bless and champion that marriage? Why or why not?

- How much of marriage really has to do not with falling in love, but with the choice to love? Are romantic feelings necessary and helpful to a happy marriage? How might our focus on romance create false expectations and become a stumbling block?

- Is it possible that God would in fact lead us to marry someone that we seem incompatible with from a practical standpoint? Why or why not? Should the head and the heart always agree in matters of love?

Tell Yourself the Truth—"Leaving Home"

A self-quiz for couples.

1. I often wish my spouse was more/less like my mom/dad.
a. agree   b. somewhat agree   c. somewhat disagree   d. disagree

2. My mate and I have arguments about our in-laws.
a. daily   b. weekly   c. occasionally   d. rarely or never

3. I can trust my spouse not to share intimate and personal information about our marriage with his/her parent/s or family members.
a. disagree   b. somewhat disagree   c. somewhat agree   d. agree

4. I continue to struggle with deep resentment and/or anger toward at least one of my parents.

a. agree   b. somewhat agree   c. somewhat disagree   d. disagree

5. I usually respect and value my spouse's advice and opinions more than my parents'.
a. disagree   b. somewhat disagree   c. somewhat agree   d. agree

6. I find myself projecting expectations or resentment onto my spouse that are probably really about my parents.
a. frequently   b. occasionally   c. rarely   d. never

7. I accuse my spouse of acting or sounding just like one of our parents.

a. daily   b. weekly   c. occasionally   d. rarely or never

8. I have forgiven my parents' failures and yet want to do things differently in my own family.
a. disagree   b. somewhat disagree   c. somewhat agree   d. agree

How did you score?

    a's = 1 point
    b's = 2 points
    c's = 3 points
    d's = 4 points

If you scored 8–15, you struggle with issues of separating emotionally from your parents and should pray about and work to improve in this area.

If you scored 16–25, a healthy separation from home is important to you, but there's still room for growth.

If you scored 26–32, you and your spouse have successfully "left home" and are at peace with your parents, free to form a strong bond in marriage.

What Else Does the Bible Say?

Read and consider other related Scriptures.

Seeking God's direction: Psalm 25:9-15; 32:8; Isaiah 42:16; John 16:13; James 1:5-8

Prayer/fleece-setting: Judges 6:36-40; Esther 4:4-17; Matthew 7:7-8; Philippians 4:6; Hebrews 4:16

Faith in God's goodness: Joshua 1:9; Psalm 37:3-7; Proverbs 3:5-6; Hebrews 10:35,38; 11

Loyalty: 1 Samuel 20:1-4; Psalm 55:12-14; Proverbs 27:6,10; John 15:12-17; 2 Timothy 1:16-18

4. Jacob, Rachel, & Leah
When Love Is Hard Work

Marriage Puzzlers

Real life questions for today:

- Today we don't have "bride-prices," but what are some modern ways that a mate might seem "costly" to us?

- What are some signs in a marriage that jealousy is out of hand? What if one mate believes that this type or degree of jealousy is warranted?

- Do couples sometimes provoke each other to jealousy on purpose? Why?

- What advice would you give to a person who felt unloved in his or her marriage?

- If our parent is mistreating our spouse in some way—e.g., insults, unfairness, gossip, criticalness—what is our duty? How can we help without getting in the middle?

Tell Yourself the Truth—"How Hard Do You Work at Love?"

A self-quiz for couples.

1. My marriage is something I don't really have to work at. It's just there.
a. agree   b. somewhat agree   c. somewhat disagree   d. disagree

2. I often go out of my way to do something extra in the way of a task to help my mate.
a. rarely or never   b. occasionally   c. weekly   d. daily

3. When my mate feels insecure or jealous, I try to find ways to make him or her feel more secure.
a. disagree   b. somewhat disagree   c. somewhat agree   d. agree

4. It gets harder each year to put time and energy into our marriage.
a. agree   b. somewhat agree   c. somewhat disagree   d. disagree

5. I am willing to make costly sacrifices myself in order to put my mate and my marriage first.

a. rarely or never   b. once in a while   c. regularly   d. frequently

6. If a marriage requires an extensive amount of effort and striving, it may mean that we married the wrong person.

a. agree   b. somewhat agree   c. somewhat disagree   d. disagree

7. I invest a lot of time and energy into my marriage without keeping score or expecting an equal return on my effort.

a. disagree   b. somewhat disagree   c. somewhat agree   d. agree

8. I work hard to find ways to have fun and "play" with my mate.

a. rarely or never   b. occasionally   c. weekly   d. daily

How did you score?

> a's = 1 point
> b's = 2 points
> c's = 3 points
> d's = 4 points

If you scored 8–15, you probably aren't working as hard at your marriage relationship as you need to. How could you improve in this area? Do you want to?

If you scored 16–25, working at marriage is important to you, but there's still room for growth. Based on your answers, what are the weak areas?

If you scored 26–32, you have invested a lot of work into your marriage and are probably seeing great results!

What Else Does the Bible Say?

Read and consider other related Scriptures.

Perseverance: Romans 5:3-4; Galatians 6:9; 2 Peter 1:5-9

Strife: Proverbs 17:1; 21:9; 30:33; James 4:1-3

Contentment: Psalm 34:14; Isaiah 26:3; 1 Timothy 6:6-8

Blessing: Psalm 29:11; Matthew 5:3-11; Romans 10:12

5. Samson & Delilah
Avoiding Selfish Pitfalls

Marriage Puzzlers

Real life questions for today:

- Should we tell our spouses anything about ourselves they want to know? Or is there a time and place for secrets? If so, under what conditions?

- What is the difference between nagging and reminding? (Do you and your spouse agree?)

- Is nagging ever effective? How can we help to change a pattern of nagging?

- When is it disloyal to discuss marriage problems, including a spouse's weaknesses, with a friend?

- Synonyms for manipulation include "maneuver," "deception," "ruse," and "trickery." When does an attempt to sway one's spouse on an important issue cross over into manipulation?

Tell Yourself the Truth—"A Matter of Loyalty"

A self-quiz for couples.

1. During the heat of an argument, I use intimate knowledge I have of my partner's faults and weaknesses to hurt him/her.
a. often   b. occasionally   c. rarely   d. never

2. Under the guise of humor or "being real," I am apt to make disparaging comments about my spouse's flaws to close friends.
a. often   b. occasionally   c. rarely   d. never

3. I encourage my partner to pursue his/her gifts and calling before God, even when this could mean less income or more inconvenience for me or my family.
a. rarely or never   b. seldom   c. usually   d. always

4. I flirt with unfaithful thoughts or I risk disloyalty in situations that I think are "safe" or won't be found out (e.g., imagining a romantic liaison; exploring adult sites on the web; etc.).

a. often   b. occasionally   c. rarely   d. never

5. I am careful not to share with others anything my spouse has told me in confidence and intended to be private.

 a. rarely or never   b. seldom   c. usually   d. always

6. I will encourage my mate to compromise what he/she thinks is a priority if I can get something I want (e.g., "Honey, why don't you skip the ushers' meeting and take me to lunch!").

a. often   b. occasionally   c. rarely   d. never

7. If the truth about something would really help my partner, and I am the best one to talk to him/her, I am willing to risk short-term upset for a long-term benefit to the person I love.

a. rarely or never   b. seldom   c. usually   d. always

8. I can identify at least one other person who is such a close friend to me and my marriage that I'm confident that he/she will intervene with the truth if he/she sees me heading into trouble.

a. no, not even one   b. possibly   c. yes, probably   d. definitely

How did you score?

> a's = 1 point
> b's = 2 points
> c's = 3 points
> d's = 4 points

Use these scores for further thinking:

If you scored 8–15, you struggle with issues of loyalty and should pray about and work to improve in this area.

If you scored 16–25, loyalty is important to you, but there's still room for growth.

If you scored 26–32, you are a very loyal spouse, and most likely this is an area of strength in your marriage.

What Else Does the Bible Say?

Read and consider other related Scriptures.

Pride: Proverbs 11:2; 12:1; 16:16-25

Nagging: Proverbs 11:22; 19:13

Immorality: 1 Corinthians 6:12-20; Colossians 3:5-9

Foolishness: Proverbs 26:11; 28:26

6. Ruth & Boaz
Shaping a Redemptive Marriage

Marriage Puzzlers

Real life questions for today:

- How important is it for both people in a marriage to feel that the other person "needs" them?

- What is the difference between the urge to rescue a spouse and the urge to help that person grow?

- What practical things can we do to help our mates recover from past hurts?

- When one spouse has many needs—emotional, physical, financial, spiritual—what are some ways the other spouse can make sure his or her own needs are met?

- How does a spouse who is trying to be a "redeemer" to his/her partner keep from taking on the role of a "parent"? How might this be a problem?

Tell Yourself the Truth—"I Need You; You Need Me"

A self-quiz for couples.

1. I believe that my mate and I bring out the best in each other.

a. rarely or never   b. occasionally   c. often   d. always

2. My mate is interested in my childhood and my earlier life, and often helps me to understand how my past affects who I am today.
a. disagree   b. somewhat disagree   c. somewhat agree   d. agree

3. My mate has my permission to say difficult things to me, to tell me the truth about myself even when that truth will be painful or challenging to me.
a. disagree   b. somewhat disagree   c. somewhat agree   d. agree

4. I've accepted the fact I have certain needs that I wish my mate could fill that he or she probably never will.

a. disagree   b. somewhat disagree   c. somewhat agree   d. agree

5. My mate and I would agree that we "need" each other equally, if only in different ways.

a. disagree   b. somewhat disagree   c. somewhat agree   d. agree

6. My mate has unrealistic expectations about which of his or her needs I can really fulfill.

a. often   b. I'm not sure   c. occasionally   d. rarely or never

7. I feel more safe, known, and accepted by my spouse than by any other person.

a. disagree   b. somewhat disagree   c. somewhat agree   d. agree

8. My mate hurts me by reminding me of my weaknesses and personal flaws.

a. often   b. I'm not sure   c. occasionally   d. rarely or never

How did you score?

>   a's = 1 point
>   b's = 2 points
>   c's = 3 points
>   d's = 4 points

If you scored 8–15, you and your spouse have some trouble in the area of meeting each other's needs. Initiate a conversation with your spouse about how the two of you might work on this area.

If you scored 16–25, you and your mate care for and try to understand each other but there's still room for growth. Based on your answers, in what areas do you see a need for improvement?

If you scored 26–32, you and your mate have a "redemptive" marriage where needs usually become opportunities for love and growth.

What Else Does the Bible Say?

Read and consider other related Scriptures.

Redemption: Jeremiah 31:10-14; Psalm 68:5; 130

Healing: Psalm 103:1-5; Isaiah 58; Mark 2:1-12

Love: Proverbs 27:5; Romans 13:8-10; 1 John 3,4

Acceptance: John 13:20; Romans 10:11-13; Hebrews 11:16

7. Hannah & Elkanah
Nurturing Spiritual Unity

Marriage Puzzlers

Real life questions for today:

- How should a couple deal with a decision when each partner believes God is saying something different?

- What is the difference between spiritual unity (or agreement) and spiritual intimacy?

- Because in lovemaking we become "one flesh," do you think a couple can reach full physical intimacy without also being spiritually intimate?

- What is the difference between making a vow such as Hannah's and trying to bargain with or manipulate God? Can you think of some ways you might try to bargain with God?

- What are some practical ways we can comfort our mates if they are in deep pain or grief? What if our mate just doesn't respond to the comfort we offer?

- It's tempting for us to judge the spiritual life of our spouse by convenient outward indicators. What might the danger of this be? For a couple who feels unevenly matched spiritually, what are some ways one could encourage the lagging spouse without slipping into judgment or manipulation?

Tell Yourself the Truth—"Becoming One in Spirit"

A self-quiz for couples.

1. Spiritual intimacy with my spouse is something I:

    a. don't often experience
    b. feel now and then
    c. have and want to keep working hard at
    d. enjoy and nurture regularly

2. My mate and I pray together.

a. rarely or never   b. occasionally   c. weekly   d. daily

3. My spouse and I share personal musings or insights on spiritual matters.
a. rarely or never   b. occasionally   c. weekly   d. daily

4. My spouse and I see eye to eye on key spiritual and values issues.
a. disagree   b. somewhat disagree   c. somewhat agree   d. agree

5. I care as much about developing spiritual intimacy with my spouse as I do about having romantic intimacy.
a. disagree   b. somewhat disagree   c. somewhat agree   d. agree

6. I care as much about developing spiritual oneness with my spouse as I do about sharing sexual intimacy.
a. disagree   b. somewhat disagree   c. somewhat agree   d. agree

7. My spouse and I enjoy ministering together spiritually (e.g., teaching, lay service, prayer and healing, music, hospitality).
a. disagree   b. somewhat disagree   c. somewhat agree   d. agree

8. The most important aspect of spiritual intimacy in my marriage is:
    a. sharing the same basic beliefs and values
    b. attending church together
    c. talking about our spiritual experiences with each other
    d. praying together

How did you score?
    a's = 1 point
    b's = 2 points
    c's = 3 points
    d's = 4 points

If you scored 8–15, you struggle with issues of spiritual intimacy and should pray about and work to improve in this area.

If you scored 16–25, spiritual intimacy is important to you, but there's still room for growth.

If you scored 26–32, you care deeply about spiritual intimacy, and most likely your partner reciprocates this desire.

What Else Does the Bible Say?

Read and consider other related Scriptures.

Spiritual unity: 1 Corinthians 7:5; 2 Corinthians 6:14; Ephesians 4:3-6

Comfort/Encouragement: 2 Corinthians 1:3-5; 1 Thessalonians 5:11

Good deeds: Hebrews 10:19-25

Prayer: Luke 11:1-13; Romans 12:12; Philippians 4:6; James 5:16

Keeping promises to God: Psalm 50:14-15; Ecclesiastes 5:1-7

Parenting: Deuteronomy 5, 6; Proverbs 1–5; Ephesians 6:1-4

8. David & His Wives
Guarding Your Heart

Marriage Puzzlers

Real life questions for today:

- What steps might a mate take whose partner is bitter toward him/her and can't seem to let go of certain old wounds?

- Are there some limits to what a human love relationship should be expected to survive in the way of separations, in-law interference, family deaths, and so forth? Explain.

- Why are our spouse's words of affirmation about our character and destiny so important to us?

- How can we distinguish between a reassuring, "I believe in you," and a possibly threatening, "I expect great things of you (and so don't disappoint me)?"

- When a couple enters marriage under a cloud of guilt, how can you help one another make a fresh start? How long do the consequences of sin last?

Tell Yourself the Truth—"Heart Safety"

A self-quiz for couples.

1. I could easily list three times my mate has hurt me deeply in the last month.

a. agree   b. somewhat agree   c. somewhat disagree   d. disagree

2. My spouse and I go to bed at night angry or fighting.

a. daily   b. weekly   c. occasionally   d. rarely or never

3. I harbor a grudge toward my spouse long after he or she thinks we've moved on.

a. frequently   b. regularly   c. once in a while   d. rarely or never

4. It gets harder each year to feel like we can make a fresh start. There's just so much water under the bridge now.

a. agree   b. somewhat agree   c. somewhat disagree   d. disagree

5. I am willing to take risks of being honest or even confrontive with my spouse in order to protect his or her integrity and walk with the Lord.

a. disagree   b. somewhat disagree   c. somewhat agree   d. agree

6. When I feel hurt by my spouse's behavior or words I tend to lash out in anger instead of saying, "I feel hurt."

a. often   b. frequently   c. occasionally   d. rarely or never

7. My spouse and I are both committed to not bringing old, past offenses into current disagreements.

a. disagree   b. somewhat disagree   c. somewhat agree   d. agree

8. I am deeply aware of my own capacity to sin in big ways, and I can identify with those who "sin grievously."

a. disagree   b. somewhat disagree   c. somewhat agree   d. agree

How did you score?

    a's = 1 point
    b's = 2 points
    c's = 3 points
    d's = 4 points

If you scored 8–15, you probably have some bitterness or other hurts of the heart to work through that are continuing to negatively affect your marriage. Are you willing to work toward healing?

If you scored 16–25, you guard your heart against bitterness, but there's still room for growth. Based on your answers, where are the weak areas?

If you scored 26–32, you have invested a lot of work into keeping your heart free of bitterness or other unresolved emotional injuries, and your marriage has benefited.

What Else Does the Bible Say?

Bitterness/unforgiveness: Proverbs 10:12; Ephesians 4:31; Colossians 3:13; James 3:11-16

The power of words/affirmation: Proverbs 12:18; Colossians 4:6; James 3

Confession of sin, repentance, and restoration: Ezra 9:1–10:17; Psalm 25; 32; 119:33-40; Hebrews 4:14-16; 1 John 1:9

9. *The Lover & the Beloved*
Celebrating the Pursuit of Intimacy

Marriage Puzzlers

Real life questions for today:

- How true is it that men are generally more interested in sex, and women in romance? If so, how do you account for this, and how does it affect your relationship?

- Is it possible for a man to be romantic without ever writing poetry, sending flowers, taking his wife on dates, or bringing her candy? If so, how? What else is romantic to a woman?

- If sexual love is to be exclusive, how about romantic attractions or thoughts? Compare the damage done by an emotional crush versus a sexual affair.

- What is the difference between trying to sexually seduce your mate and manipulating your mate? How can a spouse ask for sex without applying a disrespectful degree of pressure?

- Why do you think it is difficult for many couples to talk openly about sex when it is one of the most intimate aspects of their relationship?

- Do you believe that Christian couples in general have better sex lives than nonbelieving couples? If so, why might that be or not be? Can you argue both sides?

Tell Yourself the Truth—"Sexual Intimacy"

A self-quiz for couples.

1. Sexual pleasure and satisfaction during lovemaking is something I:

    a. don't often experience

    b. feel now and then/would like to more often

    c. usually experience

    d. experience regularly

2. My mate and I disagree or have hurt feelings over the frequency or nature of our sexual encounters.

a. often   b. I'm not sure   c. occasionally   d. rarely or never

3. My spouse and I communicate verbally during lovemaking.

a. rarely or never   b. occasionally   c. often   d. always

4. My spouse and I understand and respect what is appropriate and comfortable for each of us as far as sexual boundaries.

a. disagree   b. somewhat disagree   c. somewhat agree   d. agree

5. I care as much about my mate's satisfaction and pleasure during sex as my own.

a. disagree   b. somewhat disagree   c. somewhat agree   d. agree

6. In our marriage, one of us consistently plays the role of initiator/aggressor and the other of responder (or decliner).

a. agree   b. somewhat agree   c. somewhat disagree   d. disagree

7. Our sex life isn't static, but always improving, even if by small increments.

a. disagree   b. somewhat disagree   c. somewhat agree   d. agree

8. For me, the most important aspect of making love with my partner is:

    a. feeling like I am being a good partner, having done my "duty"
    b. satisfying my physical urges and needs
    c. feeling emotionally close to my mate
    d. expressing love and affection to my mate in the most direct and physical way I can

How did you score?

    a's = 1 point
    b's = 2 points
    c's = 3 points
    d's = 4 points

If you scored 8–15, you struggle in the area of sexual intimacy and should pray about and work to improve in this area. Initiate a conversation in a nonsexual context with your spouse about this part of your life together.

If you scored 16–25, sexual intimacy is important to you, but there's still room for growth. Based on your answers, in what areas do you see a need for improvement?

If you scored 26–32, you experience deep and ongoing intimacy and enjoyment in your sexual life with your mate.

What Else Does the Bible Say?

Read and consider other related Scriptures.

Sexuality: Genesis 2:21-25; Hebrews 13:4

Love: Jeremiah 31:3-6; John 15:9-19

Seduction: Proverbs 30:19

Purity: Psalm 34:5; 1 Corinthians 6:12-20; Philippians 4:8; Colossians 3:1-5

10. Hosea & Gomer
Reaching for Forgiveness

Marriage Puzzlers

Real life questions for today:

- Are there times when a spouse is justified in requiring an apology before forgiveness is granted?

- Should a straying spouse always be forgiven? When does God release a partner to divorce? Does that necessarily mean he/she should?

- How and when can God use a spouse's adultery for good? Can such a marriage ever be as strong?

- Studies show that Christians commit adultery as frequently as non-believers. Why do you think this is so?

- What is it about sexual unfaithfulness that makes it so incredibly destructive to a marriage?

- Which do you think is a better approach to an actively straying spouse— "tough love" that forces a choice, or a patient, wait-it-out approach?

- Why do some people have a much harder time forgiving than others? Could the way they were raised have something to do with it?

Tell Yourself the Truth—"To Forgive or Not to Forgive?"

A self-quiz for couples.

1. My spouse and I have arguments that begin over something small but then blow up into heated altercations which include references to previous offenses.

a. often   b. occasionally   c. rarely   d. never

2. I find it next to impossible to forgive my mate if he/she doesn't seem sorry or apologize for the offense.

a. agree   b. somewhat agree   c. somewhat disagree   d. disagree

3. I feel a need to punish or hurt my mate somehow before I can actually forgive him/her and let go of my own hurt.
a. often   b. sometimes   c. rarely   d. never

4. Instead of actually forgiving my mate, I sometimes try to bury or forget an offense.
a. often   b. occasionally   c. rarely   d. never

5. I typically say "I'm sorry" to my spouse (including small things like "I'm sorry I'm late").
a. rarely/never   b. a few times a month   c. weekly   d. almost daily

6. My spouse would say that I am a very forgiving person.
a. disagree   b. somewhat disagree   c. somewhat agree   d. agree

7. It is often too painful for me to make an apology to my spouse and especially to say "I was wrong."
a. agree   b. somewhat agree   c. somewhat disagree   d. disagree

8. When we argue, I listen to and affirm my partner's feelings and perspective, even if I don't like what I hear or even if my own feelings and perspective are not being fairly treated.
a. never   b. rarely   c. occasionally   d. often

How did you score?

> a's = 1 point
> b's = 2 points
> c's = 3 points
> d's = 4 points

If you scored 8-15, you find it extremely difficult to give and receive forgiveness and should pray about and seek to improve in this area.

If you scored 16-25, forgiving and receiving forgiveness is something you know how to do, but there's still room for growth.

If you scored 26-32, you have obviously worked at learning to forgive and ask forgiveness, and this is most likely a great area of strength in your marriage.

What Else Does the Bible Say?

Read and consider other related Scriptures.

Confession: Psalm 51; Psalm 139; Luke 15:21; 1 John 1:9

Forgiveness: Matthew 18:21-35; Mark 11:25; Colossians 3:13

Godly jealousy: Exodus 20:5; 2 Corinthians 11:2

Divorce: Malachi 2:16; Matthew 19:8; 1 Corinthians 7:27

Obedience to God's calling: Ezekiel 2; Philippians 2:5-13

11. *Esther & Xerxes*
Wielding Power Wisely

Marriage Puzzlers

Real life questions for today:

- When one person obviously wields more power than another in marriage, are both partners equally responsible for this arrangement? Why might a spouse *want* his or her mate to be the one in control?

- In what areas of life do you think couples struggle the most with power issues and why?

- If one mate really feels disadvantaged by a spouse's dominance in a certain area, how might he or she best handle the problem?

- Why do certain people seem to need to be in control more than others? What else might be true about their pasts or their personalities? How might fear be involved?

- What is the difference between power and control? Between decision-making and ability to influence? How does a couple know when they have a good balance of power?

- How do women and men tend to differ in the way each wields power? In what ways might power deliver a different benefit for a man than for a woman, and vice versa?

Tell Yourself the Truth—"Who's Got the Power?"

A self-quiz for couples.

1. My spouse and I work out a compromise when both of us feel strongly about an important issue or area of control.
a. rarely or never   b. occasionally   c. often   d. always

2. I try to build up my spouse and his or her sense of personal power when he or she is feeling weak, ineffective, or especially vulnerable.
a. rarely or never   b. occasionally   c. often   d. always

3. I am uncomfortable making decisions or being the one in control—I don't really want to be responsible for outcomes.

a. agree   b. somewhat agree   c. somewhat disagree   d. disagree

4. I often ask my mate for advice and input because I prefer to make decisions, even if they're only affecting me, based on both of our feelings and insights.

a. disagree   b. somewhat disagree   c. somewhat agree   d. agree

5. My mate respects my abilities and strengths and often encourages me to take the lead in those areas.

a. disagree   b. somewhat disagree   c. somewhat agree   d. agree

6. In our marriage, one of us has a more forceful personality and consistently gets his or her way.

a. agree   b. somewhat agree   c. somewhat disagree   d. disagree

7. When my spouse is in control of a decision or event that will affect us both, I feel confident in his or her abilities and choices and try to back him or her up with my support.

a. disagree   b. somewhat disagree   c. somewhat agree   d. agree

8. I feel that my mate is trying to pressure me through covert manipulation, shame, teasing, withholding information, bullying, or other means.

a. frequently   b. occasionally   c. not often   d. very rarely or never

How did you score?

        a's = 1 point
        b's = 2 points
        c's = 3 points
        d's = 4 points

If you scored 8–15, you and your mate experience a great deal of conflict concerning control and power issues and should pray about and work to improve in this area.

If you scored 16–25, sharing power is something you're pretty good at, but there's still room for growth. Based on your answers, in what areas do you see opportunities for improvement?

If you scored 26–32, you and your mate are good at sharing power and compromising with one another to the benefit of both.

What Else Does the Bible Say?

Read and consider other related Scriptures.

Humility: Philippians 2:1-18; 1 Peter 5:5; Matthew 18:4

Power: Proverbs 18:21; Zechariah 4:6; Romans 1:16; 1 Corinthians 1:18–2:5

Submission: 2 Corinthians 4:7-18; James 3:17; 1 Peter 2:13–3:17

Beauty: Proverbs 31; Ezekiel 16:8-19

12. *Joseph & Mary*
Discovering Your Destiny

Marriage Puzzlers

Real life questions for today:

- Intense spiritual experiences are often difficult to put into words, even to one we love. Why? Do you think men might have a harder time than women with this aspect of self-disclosure? If so, why? What are reasons a couple should keep trying?

- In this couple's story, the woman seems to have the most important—or at least the most apparent—spiritual role. Does this sound familiar? What are some unique challenges to a marriage when the wife is the spiritual "star" in the family?

- The Bible tells a lot of "wife can't get pregnant" stories to throw the spotlight on the important baby that is finally born—e.g., Sarah (Isaac), Rebekah (Jacob and Esau), Rachel (Joseph), and Hannah (Samuel). But in Mary's story (about Baby Jesus), it's the husband who's left on the sidelines. What do you make of this interesting "plot twist"?

Tell Yourself the Truth— "We're Reaching for God's Will Together"

A self-quiz for couples.

1. My spouse and I share the same or a similar view of what God wants us to do with our lives.
a. disagree   b. somewhat disagree   c. somewhat agree   d. agree

2. My spouse and I talk on a regular basis about how we're doing in following God's will for us, and we make adjustments as needed.
a. never   b. rarely   c. occasionally   d. often

3. My spouse and I enjoy a high level of interpersonal trust.
a. disagree   b. somewhat disagree   c. somewhat agree   d. agree

4. Like Mary and Joseph, we have at least one or two other friends who understand the priorities in our lives and help us stay on track.

a. disagree   b. somewhat disagree   c. somewhat agree   d. agree

5. We are part of a church family who help us understand and reach for God's destiny for us as a couple.

a. disagree   b. somewhat disagree   c. somewhat agree   d. agree

6. As I consider the troubles, trials, and unexpected twists we've faced as a couple, I would give us a *success rating* of:

a. terrible   b. unsatisfactory   c. passing   d. excellent

7. As I consider the troubles, trials and unexpected twists we've faced as a couple, I would rate our *degree of improvement* in how we handle these, then to now, as:

a. getting worse   b. no change   c. some improvement   d. much improved

8. My spouse and I could, humbly and thankfully, point to situations where we see clearly that God has used our marriage and home to bring help, healing, or salvation to others.

a. never   b. rarely   c. occasionally   d. often

How did you score on reaching for God's will together?

> a's = 1 point
> b's = 2 points
> c's = 3 points
> d's = 4 points

If you scored 8–15, you struggle with issues of reaching for your destiny together.

If you scored 16–25, seeking and doing God's will together is important to you, but there's still room for growth.

If you scored 26–32, you care deeply about living out God's will for you together and about building a life together to make this happen.

What Else Does the Bible Say?

Read and consider other related Scriptures.

Trusting God: Psalm 23; 56:3-4,11; Proverbs 3:5-6; 29:25

Enduring trials: 2 Corinthians 4:8-9; Hebrews 11:1–12:12; James 1:2-8

Knowing and obeying God's will: Isaiah 30:21; John 16:13-15; James 1:5-8

When plans seem to go wrong: Romans 8:28; 2 Corinthians 4:16-18; Philippians 1:6

God's destiny for His people: 1 Corinthians 1:26–2:10; Hebrews 12:1-3; 1 Peter 1-2:12

Other Books
by David and Heather Kopp

LOVE STORIES GOD TOLD

The romantic in all of us loves a love story. And we shouldn't be surprised to discover that the world's greatest love stories come from the hand of God.

In these stories retold from the Bible, we meet men and women drawn into love by a tender Creator. Like us, they're driven by courage and cowardice, they experience betrayal and bliss. And through them we gain divine inspiration for another precious love story—our own.

BABY STORIES GOD TOLD

In *Baby Stories God Told,* David and Heather Kopp share the wonder of a new birth by retelling biblical stories of babies anticipated, born, and rejoiced in.

David and Heather Kopp combine their literary talents to recreate heartwarming biblical stories that reflect the love of parents for their children and the hope that a new birth brings to our world.

ONCE UPON A ROMANCE

Noble love, true and pure, springs to life in timeless excerpts from the greatest romantic stories of all time—from *Jane Eyre* to *Little Women, Pride and Prejudice* to *Beauty and the Beast.*

In the pages of fairy tales come true we find inspiration for our own love stories—those already written and those yet to be.